E-books

OTHER TITLES IN THE TECHNOLOGY 360 SERIES:

Cell Phones

Electric Cars

Global Positioning Systems

iPod® and MP3 Players

Online Schools

Online Social Networking

Robots

Rollercoasters

Video Games

Web 2.0

TECHNOLOGY 360

E-books

BY HAL MARCOVITZ

LUCENT BOOKS
A part of Gale, Cengage Learning

GALE
CENGAGE Learning·

Detroit • New York • San Francisco • New Haven, Conn • Waterville, Maine • London

©2013 Gale, Cengage Learning

LIBRARY OF CONGRESS CATALOGING-IN-PUBLICATION DATA

Marcovitz, Hal.
   E-books / by Hal Marcovitz.
     pages cm. -- (Technology 360)
   Includes bibliographical references and index.
   ISBN 978-1-4205-0902-1
  1. Electronic books--Juvenile literature. 2. Electronic publishing--Juvenile literature. 3. Electronic book readers--Juvenile literature. 4. Books and reading--Forecasting--Juvenile literature. I. Title. II. Title: Ebooks.
   Z1033.E43M37 2013
   070.5'73--dc23   2012044958

Lucent Books
27500 Drake Rd
Farmington Hills MI 48331

ISBN-13: 978-1-4205-0902-1
ISBN-10: 1-4205-0902-0

Printed in the United States of America
1 2 3 4 5 6 7 17 16 15 14 13

CONTENTS

FOREWORD

"As we go forward, I hope we're going to continue to use technology to make really big differences in how people live and work."
—Sergey Brin, co-founder of Google

The past few decades have seen some amazing advances in technology. Many of these changes have had a direct and measureable impact on the way people live, work, and play. Communication tools, such as cell phones, satellites, and the Internet, allow people to keep in constant contact across longer distances and from the most remote places. In fields related to medicine, existing technologies—digital imaging devices, robotics and lasers, for example—are being used to redefine surgical procedures and diagnostic techniques. As technology has become more complex, however, so have the related ethical, legal, and safety issues.

Psychologist B.F. Skinner once noted that "the real problem is not whether machines think but whether men do." Recent advances in technology have, in many cases, drastically changed the way people view the world around them. They can have a conversation with someone across the globe at lightening speed, access a huge universe of information with the click of a key, or become an avatar in a virtual world of their own making. While advances like these have been viewed as a great boon in some quarters, they have also opened the door to questions about whether or not the speed of technological advancement has come at an unspoken price. A closer examination of the evolution and use of these devices provides a deeper understanding of the social, cultural and ethical implications that they may hold for our future.

Technology 360 not only explores how evolving technologies work, but also examines the short- and long-term impact of their use on society as a whole. Each volume in Technology 360 focuses on a particular invention, device or family of similar devices, exploring how the device was developed; how it works; its impact on society; and possible future uses. Volumes also contain a timeline specific to each topic, a glossary of technical terms used in the text, and a subject index. Sidebars, photos and detailed illustrations, tables, charts and graphs help further illuminate the text.

Titles in this series emphasize inventions and devices familiar to most readers, such as robotics, digital cameras, iPods, and video games. Not only will users get an easy-to-understand, "nuts and bolts" overview of these inventions, they will also learn just how much these devices have evolved. For example, in 1973 a Motorola cell phone weighed about 2 pounds (.907kg) and cost $4000.00—today, cell phones weigh only a few ounces and are inexpensive enough for every member of the family to have one. Lasers—long a staple of the industrial world—have become highly effective surgical tools, capable of reshaping the cornea of the eye and cleaning clogged arteries. Early video games were played on large machines in arcades; now, many families play games on sophisticated home systems that allow for multiple players and cross-location networking.

IMPORTANT DATES

Between 1450 and 1456

Johannes Gutenberg, a German blacksmith, creates the first printing press. The first book printed by Gutenberg is the Bible.

1991

Franklin Electronic Publishing markets the first e-reader, a device dedicated solely to the Bible. Franklin sells 50,000 electronic Bibles within six months.

1945

Computer scientist Vannevar Bush predicts in an article for *The Atlantic* that a relatively small machine can be developed capable of holding a library's worth of books.

1976

Computer engineer Ray Kurzweil develops the first optical scanner, enabling documents and book pages to be reproduced and displayed on a computer screen.

1450 **1950** **1970** **1990**

1958

Texas Instruments engineer Jack Kirby develops the first microprocessor, a tiny device that enables computers to process information faster. Also known as the silicon chip, the microprocessor leads to development of personal computers and eventually e-readers and tablets.

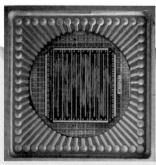

1990

The *American Heritage Dictionary* is produced on a floppy disk at a cost of $90; readers can buy a hardback version, containing twice the number of words, for about $17.

1993

Michael Crichton's science fiction novel *Jurassic Park* is sold on floppy disks.

1971

University of Illinois student Michael Hart types the Declaration of Independence into a computer at school, launching Project Gutenberg.

1995

Entrepreneur Jeff Bezos launches Amazon.com, the first online bookseller.

in the Development of E-books

2007
Amazon.com releases the Kindle, an e-reader that sells out six hours after it goes on the market.

1999
E Ink develops e-paper: a light-sensitive and oil-coated substance capable of displaying text. The product does not yet offer the resolution of characters that enables it to be used in e-readers.

2009
California approves the use of e-textbooks in classrooms.

2011
Borders, a company with five hundred bookstores in the United States, goes out of business; analysts say that competition from e-books helped bring about its downfall.

2004
Google launches Google Books, with the intention of posting the contents of every book in print on the Internet.

2000   **2003**   **2006**   **2009**   **2012**

1998
E-readers such as the SoftBook and Rocket eBook go on the market, each with memories that hold about ten books.

2010
Apple Inc. releases the iPad, the first commercially successful tablet computer. The computer's many functions include the ability to display e-books.

2000
Project Gutenberg posts its three hundredth book online.

2006
Sony Corporation markets the Sony Reader, the first e-reader available to U.S. consumers that uses e-paper.

2012
The first e-readers featuring color screens go on sale in Asian countries.

Publishing's New Frontier

According to the Nielsen Company, which tracks trends in media use, the average U.S. teenager spends more than four hours a day watching TV. That is not true, however, in the Litos household in Harrison, New York, where eleven-year-old Eliana Litos says she hardly watches TV at all. "Some weeks I completely forgot about TV," she says. "I went two weeks with only watching one show, or no shows at all."[1]

Instead, Litos spends most of her free time glued to her Nook, one of many e-readers that have flooded the consumer market during the past decade. Using the hand-held device, Litos is able to browse through online bookstores, finding titles that cost a fraction of their print versions. Downloading often only takes a few seconds.

Before buying the e-reader for her daughter, Amy Mauer-Litos says she wanted to make sure Eliana's teachers would allow her to use the device to read books for school projects. When the teachers gave their assurance that e-readers are also valuable tools for classroom work, Mauer-Litos purchased the Nook for her daughter. Mauer-Litos says, "I don't know whether it's the device itself that is appealing, or the easy access to the books, but I will tell you, we've had a lot of snow days lately, and nine times out of ten, she's in the family room reading her Nook."[2]

Readers have been able to enjoy books in electronic formats since the 1980s, but the explosion of e-books as an important segment of the publishing industry is a relatively new phenomenon. Canadian science fiction author Cory Doctorow says e-books are a good fit with the electronic culture of the twenty-first century digital age: readers can obtain books as fast as they can download them and use search features to highlight the information they need. He says, "Ebooks don't beat paper books for sophisticated typography, they can't match them for quality of paper or the smell of the glue. But just try . . . loading a thousand paper books [into a backpack]. Or searching a paper book for every instance of a character's name to find a beloved passage."[3]

By 2011, e-books still represented just 10 percent of overall book sales in the United States, but there is no

In a New York City park in 2010, a woman reads an e-book on an Amazon Kindle.

question they are the fastest-growing segment of the publishing industry. In fact, in 2011, Amazon, the nation's top online bookseller, announced that for the first time, sales of e-books on the company's website outpaced sales of printed books. According to Amazon, in 2011 it sold 105 e-books for every 100 printed books purchased by customers.

As e-books grow in popularity, they promise to become an even bigger part of the publishing industry. The *Wall Street Journal* estimates that in 2013, e-book sales will pass the $2 billion mark. The technology that makes e-books possible continues to evolve, and they are likely to become more sophisticated and colorful. Soon, readers should not be surprised if they find their favorite stories virtually jumping off their screens.

CHAPTER 1

Evolution of the E-book

E-books were not born in a computer lab in California's high-tech Silicon Valley or in a university classroom. Rather, the idea that a book could be read on a computer screen was hatched in an unlikely place: an IGA grocery store in Urbana, Illinois. That is where Michael Hart, a student at the University of Illinois, stopped to buy snacks on his way to school in 1971. Later that day, Hart planned to use his school's computer and had been giving some thought to how he would be using his time on the machine. The computer Hart would be using that day bore little resemblance to the sleek laptops, tablets, and flat-screen desktops of today. At the time Hart was enrolled at the University of Illinois, students were only allowed a brief time each week to use the school computers—huge and expensive machines, some of which cost millions of dollars. The first personal computers were still nearly a decade away from development.

Soon after shopping at the grocery store, Hart conceived the idea that would eventually lead to the development of e-books and spark a monumental change in the publishing industry. "We were just coming up on the American Bicentennial and they put faux parchment historical documents in with the groceries," he says. "So, as I fumbled through my backpack for something to eat, I found the

U.S. Declaration of Independence and had a light bulb moment. I thought for a while to see if I could figure out anything I could do with the computer that would be more important than typing in the Declaration of Independence."[4]

Transferring Words to Paper

Prior to Hart's "light bulb moment," there had not been a significant change in the way books were produced or read in more than five hundred years. The first book was printed sometime between 1450 and 1456 by Johannes Gutenberg, a German blacksmith who created what is regarded as the first printing press. The first book printed by Gutenberg was the Bible, and it is believed that he printed 180 copies, although just forty-seven are still in existence. The Gutenberg Bible was printed with movable type, meaning that after Gutenberg completed his work on the Bible he could physically change the characters to print a different book. The characters, representing letters of the German alphabet, were carved in wood or cast in metal.

A working replica of a Gutenberg press is shown at the Gutenberg Museum in Mainz, Germany. The invention of the printing press brought books to the masses.

The Father of the E-book

Michael Hart may have created the first e-books in 1971, but the idea of reading a book on a computer screen was first raised twenty-six years earlier by Vannevar Bush, a computer engineer who helped develop the atomic bomb. In 1945, Bush wrote an essay for *The Atlantic* in which he envisioned the day when a relatively small machine could hold an entire library's worth of books. "*The Encyclopedia Britannica* could be reduced to the volume of a matchbox," Bush suggested. "A library of a million volumes could be compressed into one end of a desk."

Bush's ideas were radical because at the time computers cost millions of dollars and often took up whole floors of buildings. Yet Bush envisioned a computer no bigger than a desk. He called the device a *memex*—combining the words memory and index. Wrote Bush, "A memex is a device in which an individual stores all his books, records, and communications, and which is mechanized so that it may be consulted with exceeding speed and flexibility. It is an enlarged intimate supplement to his memory."

Vannevar Bush. "As We May Think." *The Atlantic*, July 1945. www.theatlantic.com /magazine/archive/1945/07/as-we-may-think/3881.

Gutenberg's invention was a tremendous advancement. It helped spark the European Renaissance, the era in which Europe broke away from the dark and dismal medieval period, awakening people to the power and influence of art, science, and literature. Prior to the invention of the printing press, there were books, pamphlets, and other written materials available for the very few people who possessed the ability to read; indeed, archaeologists working in Egypt have unearthed papyrus scrolls that are five thousand years old. However, these written materials were copied one at a time by skilled craftsmen, working painstakingly by hand. During the medieval era, these craftsmen were often monks whose religious orders were devoted to the reproduction of written materials. With the invention of the printing press, books could be produced on a much larger scale—information could be delivered to many people, giving them the opportunities to learn to read and discover new truths about the world in which they lived.

Over the next five centuries, all books and other reading materials were produced on printing presses. By the twentieth century, the simple, hand-powered press Gutenberg invented in the 1450s bore little resemblance to the massive printing plants, some taking up whole city blocks, which could churn out thousands of newspapers, magazines, and books a day. Yet, the concept of how books and other printed materials were produced was still virtually the same as it had been in Gutenberg's day: Paper was pressed against a surface that had been inked in advance, leaving an impression of words and illustrations on the page.

The Birth of Project Gutenberg

As Hart keyboarded 1,337 words from a souvenir copy of the nation's most important document into the memory of the University of Illinois computer, he realized the significance of what he was accomplishing: If a computer could serve as an archive for a single document, it could also archive any type of printed text—including books. He would soon dedicate his life to providing computer users access to books. With a nod to history, Hart called his mission Project Gutenberg.

Over the next several months, Hart would add other historical documents to the archive: the Bill of Rights and Constitution, among others. The first two books Hart added to the archive were the King James Bible and Lewis Carroll's fairy tale, *Alice's Adventures in Wonderland*. Each document and book had to be keyboarded by hand, one letter at a time—quite similar to how the monks of the me-

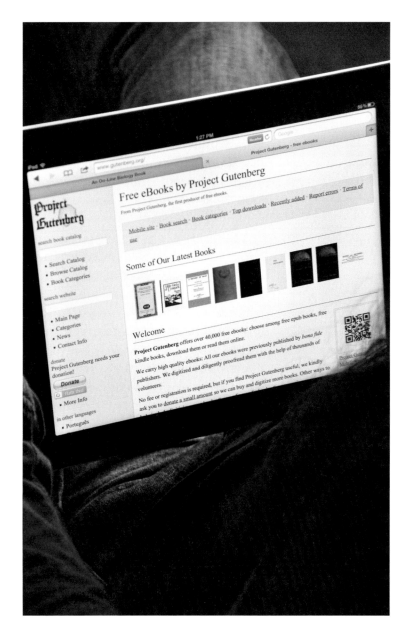

dieval period recopied books more than five hundred years before.

Hart's work could be transmitted over the Internet and read by anyone with Internet access which, at the time, was in its infancy and accessible by very few people. Nevertheless, Hart realized the potential of the Internet for archiving tremendous volumes of information as well

The Scanning Process

Google Books and Project Gutenberg employ the flatbed scanning process to convert printed pages to a format that can be read on the computer screen. The first flatbed scanner was developed in 1976 by computer engineer Ray Kurzweil, who developed optical character recognition (OCR). OCR enables a computer to recognize printed characters.

Flatbed scanning works by laying a printed page on a glass plate. Below the surface, most scanners use image capturing components known as charged couple devices (CCDs), which convert images into electrical charges. CCDs are sensitive to light, so each scanner includes a lamp that illuminates the pages to make the text and illustrations stand out. Driven by a motor, the CCD reads the content as it travels down the page under the glass plate.

Flatbed scanners are connected to computers. When the page is scanned, the OCR software in the computer accepts the electrical impulses generated by the CCD and converts the impulses into visual images.

as serving as a vehicle for sharing information with others. What could be more important than making the world's most important works of literature widely available—at no cost— to anyone with access to a computer? Hart founded Project Gutenberg with the intention of making books and other important documents available to a wide audience connected by a computer network.

The project grew slowly. At first, books had to be keyboarded by hand, but other students volunteered their time. In 1976, the first flatbed scanners were developed—these machines essentially took photographs of documents and book pages, converting them into an electronic format that could be viewed on a computer screen. The first scanners were slow, taking several minutes to read and record a single page; still, using a scanner was far quicker, and easier, than keyboarding each character in the book by hand.

Books and the Home Computer

Meanwhile, the computer culture was changing rapidly. Starting in 1958 computer technology took a dramatic turn when Texas Instruments engineer Jack Kirby developed the first microprocessor—otherwise known as the integrated circuit or silicon chip. Typically just a single centimeter square and a half-millimeter in thickness, the microprocessor could store and process tremendous amounts of information. By the 1970s, the development of the microprocessor opened the way for electronics companies to manufacture computers for consumer use.

Soon, IBM and other major electronics companies, including Commodore, Apple, and Atari, started developing computers for home use. While these companies were developing the hardware—the so-called *boxes*—other companies, such as Microsoft, were developing the software: the programs that drive the computers, make images appear on screen, instruct printers to churn out copies, cause sounds to emanate from the computer speakers, and other tasks. The home computer market exploded during the 1980s: People were using their home computers to write letters, do their homework, play games, balance their checkbooks, create art, and perform hundreds of other functions.

Jack Kirby, developer of the first microprocessor, poses surrounded by other Texas Instruments electronics in 1982.

Authors were also giving up their typewriters, turning to computers and printers to create their manuscripts. As for people using home computers to read the books written by those authors, that was not quite happening just yet.

Books on Floppy Disks

During the 1980s, home computers could hold a fraction of the data they do today. Moreover, data sharing tended to be tricky. Most data was exchanged on floppy disks, but during the 1980s the disks had a very limited amount of space—most were incapable of holding the contents of an entire book. Meanwhile, computer companies made data sharing difficult—software that could read data for IBM computers could not be installed on Apple computers. The Internet was not much help, either. At this point, most people connected to the Internet through dial-up connections, which utilized telephone lines and were notoriously slow. It could take many minutes to download information such as a single photograph. To the computer users of the 1980s, the notion of downloading the contents of a book spanning two hundred or three hundred pages was unthinkable.

Computers would eventually become more powerful. By 1990, the space available on floppy disks had improved to the point where software companies were selling dictionaries and similar reference books on floppies. It meant a student stumped for the right word to use while writing a term paper could insert the disk into the computer's floppy drive and open a virtual dictionary on the screen.

These programs could be expensive—in 1990, a hardback copy of the *American Heritage Dictionary* cost $16.95, but the company charged $90 for its floppy disk version. However, the user of the floppy version had access to many more features than were available in the hardback edition: the computer user could employ a search function and even cross-reference a companion thesaurus included on the disk (a particularly popular feature among crossword puzzle fans). On the other hand, the floppy edition included 115,000 words—about half those available in the hardback dictionary.

The Arrival of Paper

It took until the middle of the fifteenth century for Johannes Gutenberg to craft the first printing press. Historians believe the knowledge and tools to build a printing press existed for as much as one hundred years before Gutenberg built the apparatus, but there was a key ingredient missing at the time that made it impossible to print books: paper.

Until Gutenberg's age, most documents and books hand-produced by European craftsmen were composed on vellum and parchment, materials made out of animal skins—usually sheep, goats, and calves. The skins absorbed ink poorly and were too brittle to pass through a printing press. Moreover, even if the craftsmen of the day could find a way to print on animal skins, it would have taken a mass slaughter to find enough skin to fulfill a press run. "What use would it have been to be able to print with moveable type if the only medium was skin?" ask historians Lucien Febvre and Henri-Jean Martin. "It would have been impossible to invent printing had it not been for the impetus given by paper."

The process of producing paper from wood pulp was developed by the Chinese during the second century AD. It would take until the 1300s and 1400s before merchants returning from Asia brought the techniques of papermaking to European countries.

Lucien Febvre and Henri-Jean Martin. *The Coming of the Book*. New York: Verso, 1997, p. 30.

Liquid Crystal Displays

Some of the early computer reference programs were better than others. A program known as Language Master provided a dictionary and thesaurus on a floppy disk containing no fewer than 1.4 million words and their definitions. Critics found the program undesirable because to fit all that information onto a floppy disk, the software's designers included extremely brief definitions for the words. As an example, Language Master listed the definition for *demand* as "Ability and desire to buy." By checking the floppy version of the *American Heritage Dictionary*, however, a student could find a much clearer answer: "The amount of any commodity that people are ready to buy at a given time for a given price."[5]

INSIDE A LIQUID CRYSTAL DISPLAY

Liquid crystals are chemicals whose molecules can exist in a physical state between a liquid and a solid. These molecules can be manipulated by electrical current to line up in a particular way, similar to how metal shavings follow a magnet. In a basic crystal display, liquid crystals are contained in tiny cells that are "sandwiched" between two layers of polarized glass. Fluorescent light from the backlight passes through the first layer of glass and the cells, while the electrical current manipulates the molecules to allow certain levels of light to pass through the second piece of glass. The light seen through the second piece of glass is the image that a viewer sees on the screen.

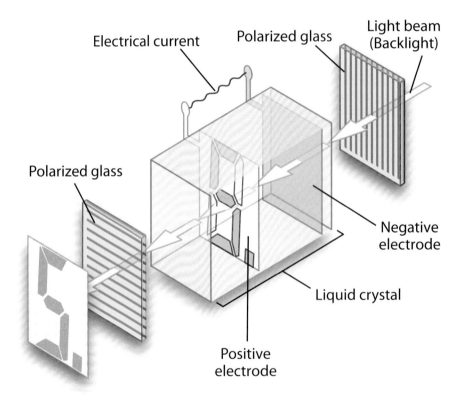

Meanwhile, some companies were developing devices dedicated to single books. In 1991, Franklin Electronic Publishers marketed a $400 handheld device dedicated solely to the Bible. The device featured a tiny screen as well as a keyboard, enabling users to search the Bible using keywords. In the first six months on the market, Franklin sold fifty thousand electronic Bibles. The company later produced an electronic version of the *Columbia Encyclopedia*, also for $400, which held as much information as the three thousand-page hardback version of the book.

However, these devices displayed their text on tiny screens that used liquid crystal display technology, or LCD. As the name suggests, LCD technology involves suspending crystals in a liquid environment; when charged with electrical current, the crystals follow the commands transmitted by the keyboard, forming characters. LCDs are commonly used in digital thermometers and similar devices that require numerical displays.

As for use in e-readers, many people found LCD displays inadequate. Readers who stared at text on the tiny LCD screens complained of eye strain. Moreover, LCD screens could not be read from certain angles, and they were impossible to read outdoors under the glare of the sun. "You would not want to read a novel on the device," wrote critic L.R. Shannon of the *New York Times* of an LCD reader he reviewed. "Its LCD screen is too small for sustained reading."[6]

The Bookman, SoftBook, and Rocket

By 1993, floppy disks had finally reached the stage where they could hold entire books. By then, at least twenty companies were producing titles on disks. These were more than just dictionaries and Bibles—titles by authors such as Michael Crichton were available. Crichton's popular science fiction novel *Jurassic Park* was among the first books to be sold on disk. Moreover, books on disks allowed users to employ the search functions of their software. Readers with poor vision could also make the type larger if they desired. Some publishers included special features on the disks— for author Ira Levin's horror novel *Sliver*, the disk included both a text and audio version of the book. Later, when CD-ROMs replaced floppy disks as the industry's principal data sharing media, publishers found they could include much more data on the CDs than they could on the floppies. In addition to the text of the book, CD-ROM versions could feature interviews with the authors as well as photographs and other art.

There were some drawbacks. If the reader owned a desktop computer, there was one place, and one place only, where the book could be read—at the computer, an obvious handicap for people who enjoyed reading before bedtime, while riding on the bus to school, or sitting in a recliner. Laptop users had a bit more mobility, but in the early 1990s laptop technology was still in its infancy, and battery life was always a concern for laptop owners.

At this point, manufacturers took their first tentative steps toward developing e-readers—unlike the Franklin versions of the Bible or encyclopedia, a user would be able to access different titles on the devices. In 1992 Franklin produced its Digital Book System, later called the Bookman. The Bookman, which is still in production, displays pages stored on plug-in *ROM cards*—small cards that hold the data for a single book. Franklin has generally restricted its market to Bibles, dictionaries, and other reference books, and continues to employ LCD technology in its screens.

By 1998, the first e-readers that resemble those in use today were introduced on the market—among the earliest models were the SoftBook and Rocket eBook. Neither were instant successes, most likely because consumers found the price range of $300 to $500 too expensive. Users also had to pay monthly fees to online bookstores that added another $240 to the price. Moreover, the early e-readers were limited to a total of ten books in their memories. Wrote *Wall Street Journal* critic Walter S. Mossberg, "Their real competition . . . isn't each other, or even traditional computers. It's the plain old paper book. And, at least in these initial versions, both electronic books are inferior in convenience and price to the dead-tree version." Mossberg added, however, that he could see e-readers improving in the future. He told readers, "I suspect these first electronic books will appeal mainly to techies, but they represent decent first efforts. As prices come down and convenience gets better, you may want one at your house."[7]

The PDF Breakthrough

Meanwhile, by the late 1990s, as home computers became more powerful and Internet speeds improved, users found more and more books available online. Hundreds of libraries in the United States and elsewhere started posting documents and books online. Many of these libraries were university-based, and the materials posted online were technical in nature; nevertheless, many computer users had

Consumers found the first e-readers, such as the Rocket eBook, too expensive.

free access to hundreds of thousands of titles. Some of these works were not technical but historical: In 1998, the British Library posted an online version of its copy of a thousand-year-old manuscript for the epic poem *Beowulf*. Two years later, the library made its copy of the Gutenberg Bible available for reading on its website.

An important breakthrough in e-publishing software occurred in 1993 when the software company Adobe Systems introduced the portable document format, or PDF. Adobe founder John Warnock envisioned the PDF as the first step toward a *paperless office*—in other words, an office where desks would not be piled high with memos, reports, receipts, bills, purchase orders, accounting ledgers, and numerous other documents. Warnock's company wanted to develop a program where all those documents could be produced in electronic versions read on computer screens. "Imagine being able to send full text and graphics documents . . . over electronic mail distribution networks," Warnock said.

The development of the PDF by John Warnock's Adobe Systems was an important breakthrough for e-publishing.

"This capability would truly change the way information is managed."[8]

Prior to the development of the PDF program, text on computers was typically read through word processing programs, which have been a staple of the data processing industry dating back to the earliest personal computers. These programs, such as Microsoft Word, WordPerfect, and Word Pro, enable writers to compose their manuscripts, identify spelling and grammar errors, set margins as well as type sizes and fonts, and perform dozens of other functions. By working with a PDF program, a page designer can take text produced by word processing programs and format it into documents that resemble typeset pages.

In addition, photographs, illustrations, headlines, and other graphics can be added at the computer as well. If a PDF could work for a sales report, it could certainly work for a book—a fact recognized first by Adobe. In 2000, Adobe purchased Glassbook, an early publisher of e-books that specialized in producing technical manuals. Adobe planned to use Glassbook to produce books in the PDF format. Soon, the concept spread to other types of books when Adobe signed contracts with the booksellers Amazon and Barnes & Noble to sell downloadable e-books as PDFs.

The World of Public Domain

Back in Urbana, Illinois, technological improvements—the development of the microprocessor, improvements in software, faster scanning technology, and the availability of the personal computer—made the job of the Project Gutenberg volunteers a lot easier. Now, volunteers could work at home on their own computers. Despite these advancements, by 2000 there were just three thousand books available to online readers through Project Gutenberg.

Indeed, Project Gutenberg found itself hampered in the production of e-books not by technological barriers or lack of volunteer help, but by federal copyright law—the measure that ensures authors and their heirs as well as book publishers have exclusive right to the use of their creative works. Generally, under law, copyrights last for the duration of the author's life plus seventy years. It means that without the permission of the authors, their heirs or publishing companies, Project Gutenberg is prohibited from reproducing these protected works for public access without compensating the holders of the copyrights. Typically, copyright holders are loath to let their books (as well as songs, movies, and other creative works) be used without receiving compensation in return. Project Gutenberg is a nonprofit organization that relies on grants and donations for its funding, so the organization does not have the resources to pay copyright holders for the rights to reproduce their books in electronic format.

Nevertheless, there is an abundance of public domain books—meaning their copyrights have expired—that are available for access by Project Gutenberg. These are the books that Project Gutenberg has chosen to archive on the Internet. Most copyright experts have determined that books published before 1923 are in the public domain and, therefore, can be reproduced without compensating the original copyright holders. By 2012, Project Gutenberg had archived more than thirty-eight thousand books that could be downloaded and read, free of charge, by anyone with an Internet connection.

Google Challenges Copyright Laws

Project Gutenberg has been very careful not to run afoul of copyright law, but others making books available online have tested the rights of authors and publishers to maintain ownership of intellectual property. Google, the Mountain View, California, company that operates the Internet's most popular search engine, commenced a bold project to scan every book in print and make them available free to all readers through its Google Books website. After all, Google founders Larry Page and Sergey Brin founded the company in 1998 with the mission to "organize the world's information and make it universally accessible and useful."[9] They believed making every book in print available online fell within the goals of their company's mission.

In addition to making online versions of the books available on its website, Google has included search features, enabling readers to find names, dates, or references to events by typing keywords into the Google Books search bar. "The Google Books project has the modest goal of scanning all of the world's books, converting them to digital form, and making them searchable and accessible,"[10] says James Crawford, director of engineering for Google Books. With considerably more resources at its disposal than Project Guttenberg (Google's estimated worth is more than $150 billion) in 2004 Google commenced the enormous task of scanning every title that has ever been published.

The company quickly found itself confronted by some angry publishers and authors, who filed a lawsuit in 2005 protesting that Google was in violation of the copyrights on their books. Representing the authors in the case was

Jon Orwant of Google is photographed with an 1800s printing press and book spines that have been cut from books that Google has scanned. Google Books makes out-of-print books freely available online.

the Authors Guild, and the book publishers were represented by the Association of American Publishers. The authors and publishers charged that readers could find free copies of their books on the Google Books website. These books were still under copyright, they charged, and therefore they were losing royalties they could be collecting if Google Books readers were buying the books in bookstores.

Crawford believes that current copyright laws do not apply to e-books. He points out that when books go out of print—meaning the publishers no longer manufacture and sell copies—the books remain copyright protected, sometimes for decades. Typically, publishers allow books to go out of print because people lose interest in the titles and, therefore, the thin profits made from the sale of the books does not justify the costs of keeping them in print. But when books are digitized, he says, they really never go out of print—they are always available, in digitized form, to be read online or downloaded. "In the days of print books the cost of a print run was sufficiently high that when books went out of print they relatively rarely came back into print," he says. "However, in the digital world we have the technical ability to make millions of out-of-print books available as ebooks."[11] Crawford questions whether authors and publishers should be entitled to royalties on e-book versions of out-of-print books since they had no plans to collect those royalties, anyway.

Google Claims Fair Use

Google responded to the lawsuits by insisting that it has *fair use* to the books, a provision under copyright law that enables students and researchers the right to use what they find in books without compensating the copyright holders. To comply with the fair use provision, Google does not scan every page of the book, but leaves several pages out of the online versions.

The authors and publishers were not satisfied, though, and proceeded with the lawsuit. In 2008, efforts to settle the lawsuit commenced, with Google offering a $125 million fund to compensate the authors and publishers for their lost royalties. In 2011, U.S. Judge Denny Chin rejected the settlement, contending that despite leaving out pages, Google was still in violation of copyright laws, and the settlement gave one very large company too much power over intellectual content.

Chin expressed a fear that such a large company could use its resources to ultimately decide which books people should and should not read. Wrote the judge, "While the digitization of books and the creation of a universal digital library would benefit many, the [proposed settlement] would simply go too far."[12] By 2012, Google was continuing to make scanned books available on the Google Books website, but the lawsuit was still active as neither side seemed able to offer an acceptable resolution to their differences.

As Google and the publishers sort out their differences over fair use, the company continues to scan books. The

Google founders Sergey Brin and Larry Page (left to right) are involved in a number of copyright lawsuits involving Google Books.

number of books available in electronic versions now numbers in the millions—Google Books alone scanned some 15 million titles by 2011. Moreover, millions of other books are available in e-book formats sold by publishers. Michael Hart, the student who envisioned it all more than forty years ago, died in 2011. Shortly before his death, Hart said, "One thing about ebooks that most people haven't thought much about is that ebooks are the very first thing we're able to have as much as we want other than air."[13] Indeed, with so many e-books available now to readers, it may be difficult for some readers to imagine a time when a book was available in print form only, with words and illustrations produced as Gutenberg devised the process—with ink and paper.

CHAPTER 2

The E-reader Revolution

I n 1997, Massachusetts Institute of Technology (MIT) professor Joseph Jacobson sat on a beach, engrossed in a book. When he came to the end of the book, Jacobson had no desire to leave the beach but found himself out of reading material. He wondered whether a small, hand-held electronic device could be developed that would hold hundreds of titles. The user would have the ability to pick and choose from an entire personal library, displaying the pages on a screen.

At the time, e-readers such as the Bookman, SoftBook, and Rocket eBook were already on the market—but they were devices with substantial limitations. They were difficult to read in the sunlight due to their LCD screens. Moreover, they were devoted to single books such as the Bible or an encyclopedia and were limited to storing no more than ten books in their tiny memories. Serious readers like Jacobson found them inadequate.

After his vacation, Jacobson returned to MIT determined to revolutionize the screens of e-readers, making them easier to read—particularly outdoors, such as at the beach where the sun would be high and bright. Jacobson and others at MIT established E Ink, a company that would develop the product envisioned by Jacobson: electronic paper—or e-paper.

The ultra-thin screen developed by E Ink revolutionized e-readers because of its advantages over LCD displays.

The product eventually developed by E Ink is composed of a thin layer of plastic film coated with gold, capable of conducting electrical current. Layered onto the film is a coating containing millions of tiny capsules, or microcapsules, filled with oil as well as floating black and white pigments. The pigments in the oil react to the electrical current that passes through the film, forming the characters of the text the e-reader user commands the device to display—in other words, the pages of a book. "I think this is extraordinarily significant," says Jacobson. "The real dream has been to have . . . electronic books that are manufactured in the way that you would manufacture a regular book."[14]

E-paper, but No E-readers

An important feature that E Ink built into the technology was a sort of electronic bookmark. Just as a reader of a print book leaves a bookmark between the pages where he or she has left off, the e-paper designers knew they had to find a way for e-readers to display the same page after the user turns off the device. The e-paper designers were able to engineer the microcapsules so the pigments would stay in the same positions even when the current is turned off.

Book publishers recognized the significance of e-paper and its capability for revolutionizing their industry. Among the first investors in E Ink was Hearst Corporation, a media company that includes a book publishing division. Hearst invested nearly $16 million in E Ink, helping provide the company with the capital it needed to develop e-paper. "This is something that people can curl up in bed with, whereas they won't curl up in bed with a device that looks like a computer and has glass and plastic and batteries," said Kenneth Bronfin, a vice president of Hearst, who envisioned the development of e-readers. "This is a device that will actually look and feel like a book."[15]

E-paper represented a tremendous step toward the development of e-readers but in 1999, when e-paper was ready to be marketed, there were no devices capable of utilizing it. At the time, the Bookman and other e-readers on the market were engineered to feature LCD displays—they could not simply change their screens to accept e-paper. Essentially, E Ink had developed a product which, at the time, could not be applied to e-books.

Moreover, E Ink executives conceded that while the creation of a new type of e-book was the ultimate goal, e-paper probably was not ready to serve as a vehicle for displaying literary text. The resolution of the characters still needed to be refined. E Ink realized that consumers would expect the next generation of e-readers to be portable, which meant the screens would have to be small. At the time, e-paper was not yet capable of producing characters that could be shrunk down to a small size and displayed on a tiny screen while still remaining readable.

BITS & BYTES
100 microns
Diameter of a single microcapsule employed in e-paper—roughly the size of a period at the end of a sentence.

ELECTRONIC PAPER AND INK

Devices that use electronic paper may also be called electrophoretic displays because they use electrophoresis, a technology that allows one to move tiny particles through a liquid substance. Most displays include a thin layer of film that holds millions of microcapsules (each so tiny that they are comparable to the diameter of a human hair!). Within each microcapsule negatively charged black particles and positively charged white particles are suspended in clear fluid. When a positive electrical current is applied to the cell, the white particles move to the top of the capsule to make the location of the paper appear white; a negative current will bring the black particles to the top to make the screen black. Electronic readers control hundreds of these microcapsules to display characters and letters onscreen.

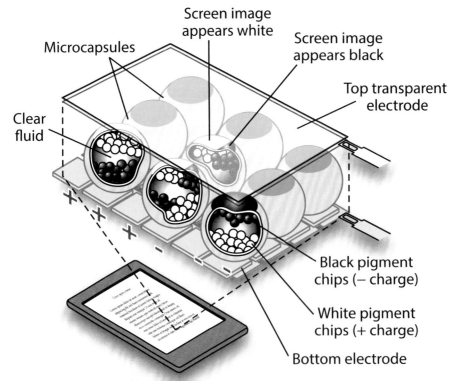

Microcapsules

Screen image appears white

Screen image appears black

Top transparent electrode

Clear fluid

Black pigment chips (− charge)

White pigment chips (+ charge)

Bottom electrode

Meanwhile, some experts doubted that readers would accept e-paper as a viable medium for displaying the text of a book. As e-paper was under development, Nicholas Sheridon, a senior research fellow at Xerox Corporation, said, "You get a pretty good display on a modern computer terminal, but it's just much nicer to read it on paper. You can never do better than paper. I don't actually know why. It's been around for a few thousand years, so the collective unconsciousness of mankind has now been directed towards liking it." Another skeptic was Stewart Hough, vice president of Cambridge Display Technology (CDT), a company headquartered in Great Britain that developed an upgrade to LCD technology. He said, "Being able to demonstrate [e-paper] at a lab or a trade show is one thing. Supplanting the world's current infrastructure of printed materials is another. If you look at how pervasive printed publications are in the world, the ability of displays to replace that massive infrastructure will take decades and decades, just by the sheer volume of it."[16]

E-paper in Department Stores

As E Ink worked toward improving the resolution of its e-paper text, and waited for the electronics companies to develop e-readers capable to displaying e-paper, the company found other uses for the product. Retail stores were among E Ink's first customers. By 1999, shoppers at J.C. Penney department stores started noticing a different type of sign advertising prices and other details about the merchandise they found on store's racks. Electronic signs featuring messages displayed in e-paper had been stationed throughout the stores, providing information to shoppers.

Rather than having new signs printed each time prices changed or new merchandise was introduced onto the sales floors, a single worker in the store's office could use a computer to change the messages and prices the store would need to convey to the customers. Moreover, the messages scrolled across the signs, providing a lot more information than shoppers were used to seeing on printed placards. There was no need to wire all the signs together—the messages traveled from the store computer to the electronic signs through a wireless link. "It's a powerful idea—having computers automatically update the signs,"[17] said Barrett Comiskey, one of the founders of E Ink.

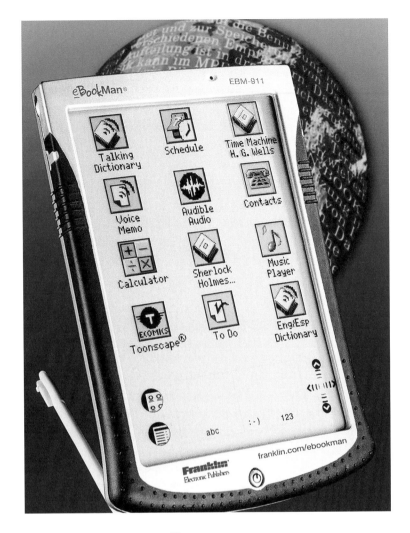

The eBookMan was one of the early e-readers that failed to catch on with the public.

Not User Friendly

Meanwhile, the world's electronics companies worked toward developing the next generation of e-readers. By the early years of the 2000s, companies such as Gemstar, RCA, GoReader, and Franklin were all working on new versions of e-readers. For the most part, these new versions of e-readers failed to catch on with consumers. Most employed LCD technology; moreover, many of the new generation e-readers had short battery lives—the batteries had to be recharged, or replaced, after a few hours of use.

In 2002, writers for the publication *Library Journal* reviewed two e-readers: the REB 1100, a device produced in a joint venture by Gemstar and RCA, and the Franklin eBookMan. The reviewers had this to say about the e-readers they tested:

> The process of registering, purchasing, and loading *Winesburg, Ohio* (an anthology of short stories by Sherwood Anderson) took approximately one hour for each REB1100 device. First, the e-book itself must be registered via a built-in modem. Then the content for that particular device had to be purchased and downloaded. . . .
>
> Registering the Franklin eBookMan and loading *The Awakening* (a novel by Kate Chopin) on the . . . devices turned out to be even more time-consuming and frustrating. The eBookMan devices were shipped with nonrechargeable batteries and no preloaded operating system. [Users] had to visit the Franklin Web site and register each device, then download the operating system. The process of loading, registering, and generally preparing these devices for use . . . continues to be far too cumbersome.[18]

When the reviewers complained to Franklin that the batteries for the eBookMan died too quickly, the company suggested readers could always use the device's AC adapter, plugging the device into a wall receptacle and running the e-reader on house current. "Of course," the reviewers noted, "this somewhat deflected one goal of the project—to provide . . . portable reading devices."[19]

Another drawback was price. The REB 1100 retailed for $300. "The high cost of handheld devices . . . is a primary concern shared by many industry members," wrote *Publishers Weekly*, the trade journal for the book publishing industry. "Virtually everyone *Publishers Weekly* spoke with was emphatic that the price of e-book readers must come down quickly."[20]

Debut of the LIBRIé

In 2004 the first version of the modern e-reader was introduced to consumers when Sony Corporation released its LIBRIé e-reader. The LIBRIé was the first device to feature

E Ink's e-paper. Since 1999, when E Ink first developed e-paper, the company had been working to resolve its resolution problems and finally produced a version that could display readable text on a very small screen. The LIBRIé weighed a mere 8.5 ounces (241 g) and measured just 5 inches (12.7 cm) by 7.5 inches (19 cm) with a width of a half-inch (1.3 cm). In fact, the e-reader was smaller than the 138-page printed manual Sony included with the device. Technology director for E Ink, Paul Drzaic, said, "We're talking about something that would be the first real change to the technology of the book in 500 years."[21]

Indeed, critics found the LIBRIé far more user friendly than the previous generation of devices. Reviewing the LIBRIé for the *Wall Street Journal*, technology writer Phred Dvorak wrote, "I took the LIBRIé on a coffee run—down a dim hallway, into the elevator and out in the bright sunlight—reading comfortably all the way. It also let me enlarge the text size up to 200 percent and has a set of built-in dictionaries for easy reference."[22]

The designers of the LIBRIé were certainly mindful of the drawbacks of the previous generation of e-readers—mainly the fact that the LCD screens made reading the devices difficult in bright sunlight. They overcame that handicap by designing the devices so they would not be backlit, similar to how computer monitor screens and laptop screens are lit from inside. Also, the e-paper developed by E Ink took very little electricity to make it function; therefore, the battery life of the LIBRIé was much longer than the REB 1100 and the eBookMan. In fact, the LIBRIé ran on four AAA batteries, which supplied enough power for the user to read ten thousand pages.

Still, the LIBRIé was not perfect. Dvorak found the response times slow. "'Turning' a page takes a full second, and using . . . the cursor through menus is frustrating," he wrote. "It's tolerable if you're chugging through a story from start to finish, but returning to a section you've read before is a real slog."[23] For U.S. readers, there was another

The Sony LIBRIé was the first e-reader to use E Ink. It was only available in Japan.

の節を抜いて、深く埋めた中から水が湧き出て、そこいらの稲に水がかかる仕掛であった。その時分はどんな仕掛か知らぬから、石や棒ちぎれをぎゅうぎゅう井戸の中へ挿し込んで、水が出なくなったのを見届けて、うちへ帰って飯を食っていたら、古川が真赤になって怒鳴り込んで来た。慥か償金を出して済んだ様である。

おやじは些ともおれを可愛がってくれなかった。母は兄ばかり贔負にしていた。この兄はやに色が白くって、芝居の真似をして女形になるのが好きだった。おれを見る度にこいつはどうせ碌なものにはならないと、おやじが云った。乱暴で乱暴で行く先が案じられると母が云った。成程碌なものにはならない。御覧の通りの始末である。行く先が案じられたのも無理はない。只懲役に行

かないで生きているばかりである。

母が病気で死ぬ二三日前台所で宙返りをしてへっついの角で肋骨を撲って大に痛かった。母が大層怒って、御前の様なものの

Author Dan Brown promotes the Sony Reader at the 2006 Consumer Electronics Show. His novel The DaVinci Code *was the first bestselling print book available for downloading from Sony.*

significant drawback of the LIBRIé: It was available for sale in Japan, only. It would take another two years before U.S. readers would be able to read an e-book on e-paper, the way Jacobson had envisioned the concept nearly a decade earlier.

The Kindle Catches Fire

In 2006, Sony introduced the device to the U.S. market under a new name: the Sony Reader. Sony's new version included several improvements over the LIBRIé. The response time had been speeded up; also, Sony found a new way to power its e-reader. Instead of employing disposable AAA batteries, the Sony Reader features a single battery rechargeable through the user's computer.

The Sony Reader was still somewhat pricey, retailing for $299. To sell books, Sony established its own online bookstore, making deals with publishers to make their print versions available in e-book formats. To access the bookstore, users connect their Sony Readers to their home computers, download the books, and then transfer them to their e-readers. The first bestselling print book available for download from Sony's online store was *The Da Vinci Code*, a mystery of murder and intrigue at the Vatican by author Dan Brown. (It was hardly a coincidence that the film version of *The Da Vinci Code* was released just as the Sony Readers were hitting the U.S. market. The film starring Tom Hanks was produced by Sony's movie division.)

By the time Sony established its online bookstore, there was already a huge presence in the U.S. online book market: Amazon.com. Amazon had been selling print books online since 1995. Its founder, Jeff Bezos, was well aware of the potential of e-books and had previously added PDF versions to his company's inventory. In 2004, Bezos started pursuing the notion of selling an e-reader. He established a new division of the company—Lab 126—to develop the device.

Amazon unveiled its new e-reader in late 2007—in time for the beginning of the holiday shopping season. The device was named the Kindle, a term suggesting the "crackling ignition of knowledge."[24] The Kindle could archive up to two hundred books and had a major advantage over the Sony Reader: Kindle owners had access to Amazon's vast inventory of e-books. In fact, there was no need to connect the Kindle to a home computer—a wireless connection linked the e-reader directly with the Amazon website. "This is really a reading service," Bezos said. "The store is right on the device. You can't out-book the book. You have to find things that you could do with this device that you could never do with a physical book. The idea [is] you could be on a train, in a car, lying in your bed and 60 seconds later have a new book."[25]

The Kindle went on sale on November 19, 2007 and—despite a cost of $399—sold out in less than six hours. It took another five months before the company was able to resume sales. Among e-readers, the Kindle has clearly emerged as the market leader. In late 2011, during the height of the holiday shopping season, company officials acknowledged that more than a million Kindles were selling each week. The robust sales were no doubt thanks in large part to the company's decision to lower the Kindle's price. By 2011 Amazon had dropped the price for the Kindle e-reader to $139; a year later, Amazon dropped the price again to a mere $79.

E-books Arrive on Tablet Computers

As the Kindle hit the market, other companies were also anxious to the join the e-reader revolution. Two major bookstore chains marketed their own e-readers: Barnes & Noble licensed its e-reader, the Nook, while Borders sold Kobo e-readers, a device manufactured by the Japanese electronics company Rakuten. By 2012, some thirty companies in the United States and elsewhere were manufacturing their own e-readers.

Most e-readers employ e-paper and function similarly: Owners are able to access online bookstores, download the e-books of their choice, and archive them in e-reader memories capable of storing hundreds of books. If a person does not own an e-reader and still wants to read a book in its e-version, software is available from online booksellers enabling the reader to download the book onto his or her home computer. However, when it comes to reading e-books on computer screens, owners face the same limitations they have always faced—home computers cannot be taken onto the bus, airplane, or a favorite easy chair. Certainly, laptop computers offer a measure of mobility but by the early 2000s computer companies started envisioning a new generation of mobile computers, known as *tablets*, that would be small enough to be held in one hand—just as a book could be held in one hand. In 2002,

Microsoft introduced the Tablet PC. Instead of a keyboard, users employed an electronic pen to transmit commands to the screen—although a keyboard was available as an accessory. The original tablets were heavy—they weighed about 3 pounds (1,360 g) and measured about 8.5 inches (21.6 cm) by 11 inches (28 cm). They were also expensive (about

The Innovative Spirit of Jeff Bezos

As a boy, Jeff Bezos spent his summers on his grandparents' ranch in rural Cotulla, Texas, an experience Bezos says gave him a taste for innovation. According to Bezos, whenever a piece of equipment broke down, his grandfather had to find innovative ways to repair it because replacement parts and people with technical expertise were often not available. Among Bezos's heroes is inventor Thomas Edison. "Edison, of course, for a little kid and probably for adults, too, is not only the symbol of [innovation] but the actual fact of that—the incredible inventor," says Bezos.

After graduating from Princeton University with a degree in computer science, Bezos found a job as a financial analyst on Wall Street in New York. During his idle moments, Bezos would surf the Internet, discovering that there was very little for sale online. At the time, people too busy to go to the store shopped by catalog, sending order forms to the ven-

dors and receiving their products in the mail. In 1994, Bezos conceived Amazon.com as an online catalog, turning to books as the first product his new website offered for sale. Eventually, Amazon added other products, and in 2011 the company reported sales of more than $48 billion.

Quoted in Academy of Achievement. "Jeff Bezos." May 4, 2001. www.achievement.org/autodoc/page/bez0int-1.

Jeff Bezos, the founder of Amazon, is credited with—and blamed for—revolutionizing the book business.

$1,500) and short on battery life—the charge lasted about two hours. Other companies, including Hewlett-Packard, Samsung, Toshiba, and Acer jumped into the tablet market as well, but none featured significant improvements over

Becoming a Computer-Aided Designer

Job Description: E-readers, tablet computers, and many other consumer products are designed by professionals on computers using software known as computer-aided design, or CAD. These professionals do not design the electronics inside the device or the software that makes them run, but rather the product itself—a very important function given that consumers often base their buying decisions on aesthetics, or how the product looks. CAD programs replace the old drafting tables and drawing equipment such as T-squares and triangles. Working with CAD programs, designers can provide three-dimensional renderings of the products.

Education: CAD designers are generally graduates of university art schools who have earned bachelor's degrees. Master's degree programs in CAD include instruction in engineering.

Qualifications: CAD designers must have a talent in art. To be accepted into a CAD design program, students must show talent in drawing, painting, graphic arts, and similar areas of artistic expression.

Additional Information: CAD professionals are able to design most any type of consumer product from earrings to refrigerators. Many CAD designers also find employment in non-consumer-oriented businesses that require designs for industrial machines and the parts that make them work.

Average Salary: About $58,000 a year.

Microsoft's Tablet PC. Consumers showed little interest, and these early tablets soon disappeared from the market.

In 2010, tablets were reborn when Apple Inc., the computer company that revolutionized the personal computer in the 1970s, introduced a new version of the device. Company co-founder Steve Jobs envisioned a new generation of mobile computers that would have a major impact on the e-book market. The Apple version was smaller than the devices produced by Microsoft and the other early tablet producers. Moreover, it could be connected wirelessly to the Internet and taken anywhere. Jobs believed the tablet could perform virtually every function a desktop or laptop computer is capable of performing—including downloading and displaying an e-book.

The first version of Apple's iPad was introduced in 2010. It was smaller than the Microsoft version, measuring 9.5 inches (24 cm) by 7.5 inches (19 cm) with a width of about a half-inch (1.3 cm) and lighter as well—it weighed about 1.5 pounds (680 g), roughly the size and weight of a

The Apple iPad was an instant hit with consumers. Hundreds of people lined up to be among the first to purchase one when it was introduced in 2010.

How Does Touchscreen Technology Work?

The e-book applications available on tablet computers employ touchscreen technology, meaning a user does not need to use a trackpad or a mouse—functions are performed by sweeping a finger across the screen. Some touchscreens feature a glass panel covering two electronically-charged metallic surfaces lying face-to-face. When the screen is touched, the two metallic surfaces feel the pressure and make contact. This pressure sends an electrical signal to the computer, which translates the touch into a command. This version of the touchscreen is known as a resistive screen because the screen reacts to pressure from the finger.

Other tablet computers feature a single electrified metallic layer under the glass panel. When the user touches the screen, some of the current passes through the glass into the user's finger. (The electrical charge is extremely slight and incapable of shocking the user.) When the charge is transferred, the computer interprets the loss in power as a command and carries out the function the user desires. This type of screen is known as a capacitive screen. In electronics, capacitance is a term used to describe the storage of an electrical charge. Essentially, the screen is storing the charge until it is drawn off by the user's finger.

hardback book. In 2010, Apple sold nearly 15 million iPads. When owners turned on the devices, they found the Apple Bookshelf application available on their screens, giving them access to e-books for sale through the company's iTunes store. Soon after the introduction of the iPad, companies such as Hewlett Packard, Motorola, Lenovo, Google, Sony, and BlackBerry brought their own tablet computers onto the market as well.

There are two types of common touchscreen technologies in use today: resistive and capacitive. Both screens translate touch into commands, but how the screens determine and interpret that contact differs. Resistive screens rely on pressure from either a person's finger or a stylus tool to capture information. Capacitive screens when touched send extremely minor electrical charges to the user's finger and interpret the associated power loss as a command.

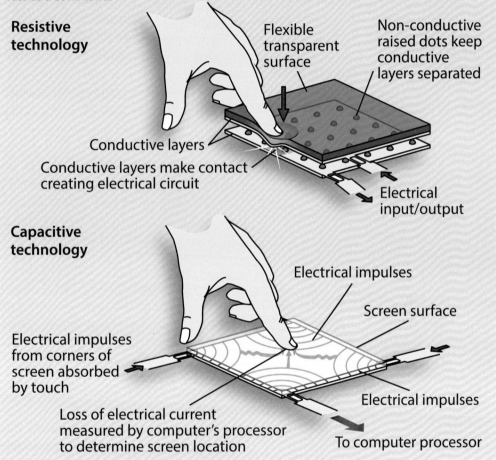

Resistive technology

Flexible transparent surface

Non-conductive raised dots keep conductive layers separated

Conductive layers

Conductive layers make contact creating electrical circuit

Electrical input/output

Capacitive technology

Electrical impulses

Screen surface

Electrical impulses from corners of screen absorbed by touch

Loss of electrical current measured by computer's processor to determine screen location

Electrical impulses

To computer processor

Touchscreen Technology

When used as an e-reader, a tablet computer displays a replica of the printed page. To turn the page, the reader employs touchscreen technology, sweeping his or her finger across the screen. Essentially, the e-book page is an animation of the printed page, controlled by the reader. Therefore, when the tablet computer is used as an e-reader, it means that e-paper is no longer a vital component of the technology.

Jobs, who died in 2011, believed owners would find tablets far more preferable than e-readers because they would be able to do much more than simply display the pages of the book. Tablet owners are able to access the Internet, stream video content, take photographs, read their e-mail, download music, and play games. "I'm sure there will always be dedicated devices," Jobs said of e-readers, "and they may have a few advantages in doing just one thing. But I think the general-purpose devices will win the day."[26] Bezos heeded that message and, in 2011, introduced a tablet version of Amazon's e-reader known as the Kindle Fire. Barnes & Noble also introduced a tablet version of the Nook.

Still, the e-reader versions of the Kindle, Nook, and similar models remain on the market and, given their low price—compared to the prices of tablets which typically cost several hundred dollars—it is likely that dedicated e-readers will remain a part of the e-book market for many years to come.

Readers Have a Library at Their Fingertips

Today's e-readers—whether they employ e-paper or touchscreen technology—are certainly vast improvements over the models first introduced a generation ago. E-readers have evolved from featuring LCD screens and tiny memories dedicated to single books such as the Bible or a dictionary, to high-tech devices capable of archiving hundreds of titles. Indeed, in 2012, Barnes & Noble introduced a version of the Nook with enough memory to archive one thousand books. Innovators like Jacobson, Bezos, Jobs, and others recognized the potential of a device that could place a virtual library at the fingertips of a user. Nevertheless, every scientist, engineer, and entrepreneur who has participated in the e-reader revolution has recognized that without books, and the people who read and write them, e-readers would serve no purpose. "The book," says Bezos, "just turns out to be an incredible device."[27]

CHAPTER 3

How Are E-books Changing the Way People Read?

Annie Proulx is one of the most successful authors in the United States. Her novel, *The Shipping News*, was awarded the Pulitzer Prize for fiction and spent several weeks on the *New York Times* bestseller list following the book's release in 1993. Her short story, "Brokeback Mountain," was adapted into an Academy Award-winning film starring Jake Gyllenhaal and the late Heath Ledger.

With those credentials, Proulx may know a lot about writing, but she may have less knowledge about how her books are read. In 1994, as the early e-readers started appearing on store shelves, Proulx had this to say about e-books: "Nobody is going to sit down and read a novel on a twitchy little screen. Ever."[28]

Time has proven her wrong. In the years since Proulx made that bold prediction, the Kindle, Nook, and other "twitchy little screens" have revolutionized the book industry.

The Battle of Print vs. E-book

In fact, some of the e-books sold by Amazon and other online booksellers include titles by Proulx. Among her books available in e-book format are *The Shipping News* and *Close Range: Wyoming Stories*, an anthology that in-

A father and son enjoy flipping through a book together. Many readers still prefer the experience of a paper book.

cludes "Brokeback Mountain." Obviously, many readers—including lovers of Proulx's fiction—have embraced the e-book format. According to the Association of American Publishers, in 2010 booksellers sold some 114 million e-books.

But not all readers have taken so easily to e-books. Auriane and Sebastien de Halleux, residents of San Francisco, California, are both avid readers. Both of them pored through the crime thriller *The Girl with the Dragon Tattoo*, engrossed by author Stieg Larsson's story of a journalist unraveling a forty-year-old mystery. While Sebastien

Engaging Young Readers with Smartphones

Book publishers find that despite young people's familiarity with electronic devices such as computers and MP3 players, they represent an age group that does not tend to buy a lot of e-books. A 2012 study by the market research firm R.R. Bowker found that 85 percent of children's books are bought in bookstores on impulse by parents. As for teens, Bowker reported that 66 percent prefer print books over e-books. "Teens like using social technology to discuss and share things with their friends, and e-books at this point are not a social technology," reports the website PaidContent.org. "An increasing number of teens surveyed say there are too many restrictions on using e-books:

14 percent said so in 2011, compared to 6 percent in 2010."

To convince more teens to read e-books, publishers and booksellers are making e-books accessible on smartphones—a favorite device among teens. In 2009, Google and Amazon both made e-book applications available for smartphones. Google's app makes some 1.5 million Google books downloadable onto smartphones, while Amazon's app makes its entire e-book inventory of 950,000 titles available to smartphone owners.

Laura Hazard Owen. "New Stats: Kids Find E-books 'Fun and Cool,' But Teens Are Still Reluctant." Paid Content.org, January 23, 2012. http://paidcontent.org /2012/01/23/419-new-stats-kids-find-e-books-fun-and -cool-but-teens-are-still-reluctant.

read the novel on his iPad, his wife insisted on reading the print version. "She talks about the smell of the paper and the feeling of holding it in your hands,"[29] says Sebastien.

Other members of the de Halleux family have weighed in on the topic of print vs. e-book. The couple reads storybooks to their three-year-old son Tristan—*Winnie the Pooh* is a favorite. Auriane insists on reading the print version to the boy, but Sebastien has downloaded a copy of A.A. Milne's classic and reads the iPad version to Tristan. Sebastien thinks Tristan prefers *Winnie the Pooh* on the iPad because the tablet enables the child to enlarge the illustrations. "He really likes it because you can zoom in on things,"[30] says Sebastien. Sebastien's parents are also avid readers. His father enjoys reading print versions while his mother prefers to read books on her e-reader because her eyesight is failing and the e-reader allows her to enlarge the type.

The dispute in the de Halleux family is not unusual. Across the United States, some people have gotten very used to reading books on their e-readers while others find it difficult to follow the text on an electronic device. Jim Hanas, a writer who lives in New York City, says he resisted e-books for a long time but finally concluded that there is little difference between reading a book in print and reading a book on a screen. "It's kind of amazing to see people still going through the stages of [belief] that books are going away, saying they like the way books feel and smell," he says. "I was there, but I'm past that now."[31]

Page Numbers Are Irrelevant

When e-readers such as the Kindle, Nook, and Sony Reader entered the market, they introduced a feature known as *reflowable text*, which enables readers to change the font or adjust the text size, margins, and spacing between the lines. Therefore, readers can configure the pages into the formats they are most comfortable reading. In a printed book the publisher, graphic artist, and other professionals select the visual features. These decisions are often based on cost—the publisher has to be mindful of how much paper has to be purchased and other expenses associated with publishing a manuscript in print form. Even in a PDF-formatted e-book, although the user can enlarge or shrink the page on a computer screen, he or she is still reading a digitized version of a printed page and has no power to make real changes to the look of the page.

Of course, when a reader tinkers with the size and style of the type, making it larger, fewer words appear on the screen. If there are fewer words on the

In 2012 Apple announced iBooks 2, a new free app featuring iPad interactive textbooks, such as Life on Earth.

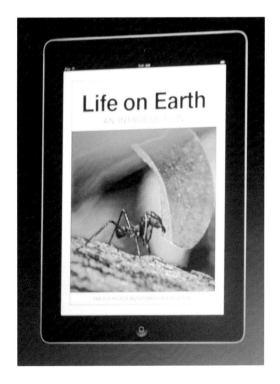

screen, the e-reader must compensate by adding pages to the book. Therefore, the reflowable text feature means the original page numbers a reader might find in the print version are irrelevant. Amazon, Sony, and other e-reader makers have compensated for the lack of page numbers by inserting *location numbers* that correspond to the text on the screen. A location number may inform a reader, for example, that he or she is at location 156 of 483 in a particular book.

Location numbers could total in the thousands, depending on the type size selected by the reader, but at least they provide readers with a reference point, marking their places in the books. The devices also tell readers how far along they have read, giving them an ongoing progress report in the form of a numerical percentage. A reader at location 667 of 1,000 is informed, at the bottom of the screen, that he or she has progressed 67 percent of the way through the book.

Where Are the Footnotes?

Whether page numbers or location numbers appear at the bottom of the page, most casual readers do not seem to mind; however, readers with more serious purposes have been troubled by the reflowable text feature. Students with assigned reading may have been given permission to read the books on their e-readers, but when teachers want to discuss a particular episode in the book, it may be a challenge for the students who read the e-book versions to find the page. As for students writing term papers—or university graduate students working on research projects—how are they to tackle the problem of adding footnotes or other citations that require them to reference specific page numbers unavailable in their e-books? Technology writer David Pogue, who reviewed the Kindle for the *New York Times*, says, "This system causes headaches for anyone who has to make specific citations: a student writing a paper, for exam-

Flipping Through an E-book

Tablet computers and e-readers enable users to turn pages, but they cannot flip through a book and shuffle through dozens of pages at a time. In 2012, software engineers at the Korea Advanced Institute of Science and Technology (KAIST) in Daejeon, South Korea, unveiled an application for tablet users that would enable them to rifle through pages of an e-book as though they are flipping through the pages of a print copy. Moreover, the application enables a user to place a finger on a specific page as a bookmark and then continue flipping.

The program, known as the Smart E-book System, works by causing a tablet or smartphone to recognize *touch and entry* finger movements on the circumference of the device, beyond the screen. This area of the device is known as the bezel molding. "Users can readily flip the pages of an e-book from the start-up screen without entering any function keys or touching the screen," KAIST says in a news release announcing the development of the software.

Korea Advanced Institute of Science and Technology. "KAIST's Smart E-book System More Convenient Than Paper-Based Books." January 10, 2012. www.kaist .edu/english/01_about/06_news_01.php?req_P=bv&req_BIDX=10&req_BNM =ed_news&pt=17&req_VI=3578#content.

ple, a teacher giving reading assignments, or someone trying to follow along at a book club."[32]

Many nonfiction authors stress the importance of footnotes. But e-reader software typically moves footnotes to the ends of the e-books, meaning that the reader has to run through commands to jump back and forth through the text. Author Alexandra Horowitz was shocked when she saw an e-book version of her book on raising dogs, *Inside of a Dog: What Dogs See, Smell, and Know*. In the print version, she added several footnotes, including a footnote warning readers not to feed grapes to their dogs because grapes are believed to be toxic to some dogs. In the e-book version, her footnotes had been moved to the end of the

An Arizona State University student uses a Kindle in the library. Sometimes e-textbooks can be frustrating when trying to locate footnotes or specific sections in a book.

book making it less likely, she fears, that people will see them. "If footnotes are at risk of going unread, endnotes are even more so," she says. "All this is discouraging for a champion of footnotes like myself. The footnotes are among the first things I look at when I pull a book from a store shelf."[33]

Technology writer Peter Meyers says he also fears that many people who read nonfiction books on e-readers ignore the footnotes. "Footnotes have got to be one of the more frustrating aspects of ebooks today," he says. "The point is: in an age of ever increasing distractions and information temptations, we need to minimize obstacles to good reading flow—especially those that occur within the document itself."[34]

Turning E-pages

Eventually, some e-reader designers recognized the need for page numbers and made some improvements in later models—providing readers with applications they could use to add page numbers that correspond with the page numbers found in the printed versions. Still, critics like Pogue have found the software fixes far from perfect. On tablets, for example, Pogue finds that when he enlarges the type and swipes his finger to turn the page, the page numbers do not always change—obviously, because the text he is reading still corresponds to the text found in the print copy. Still, he says, when a reader turns a page it is hard getting used to the fact that the page number will not always change as well. "The real page numbers, of course, may display some weirdness," Pogue says. "You might swipe your finger to 'turn the page' on your [tablet], but the page number won't change."[35]

For some Kindle e-reader models, Amazon tried another way to fix the page numbering system: It provided a separate application on the device that creates a field on the screen, giving readers the true page number regardless of how much they may have enlarged the type or otherwise altered the design of the page.

Turning the page on a Kindle has offered a far different challenge to Nicholson Baker. The author of such novels as *The Anthologist* and *The Mezzanine*, Baker purchased his Kindle in 2009 and soon found the e-reader awkward to use. Baker says that when he reads a printed book, his hand unconsciously creeps to the top right corner of the page, preparing to turn the page as his eyes approach the final few lines.

As his eye nears the last line of the Kindle page, Baker finds himself pressing the Next Page button before he has finished reading the page. He says, "I began pressing the Next Page clicker more and more eagerly, so eagerly that my habit of page turning, learned from years of reading—which is to reach for the page corner a little early to prepare for the movement—kicked in unconsciously. I clicked Next Page as I reached the beginning of the last line, and the page flashed to black and changed before I'd read it all."[36]

Reading from Start to Finish

On some Kindle models, Baker does have one option if he cannot adjust to pressing the Next Page button at the precise moment he actually needs to turn the page. Some e-readers can be commanded to turn the pages for their owners. In fact, some models of the Kindle as well as other e-readers are equipped with headphones and tiny speakers and can provide an audio version of the book on command.

As for Baker, he still is not sure an e-reader is right for him. Baker says e-readers are designed so that the user reads the e-book from start to finish—which is, after all, the intention of most authors. He points out, though, that many readers do not generally read books that way: They tend to skip around or put them down for several weeks or months or even longer, returning to the books at later dates. He wonders whether the cost of an e-reader would prompt some readers to change their habits and finish the e-books they download. "Maybe the Kindle [is] something expensive that, when you commit to it, forces you to do more of whatever it is you think you should be doing more of."[37]

Another complication for some readers is the location of the page-turning button on many e-reader models. Many of the manufacturers have placed the page-turning button on the right-side of the device, which makes sense for right-handed people. Left-handed people, however, are forced to experience a moment of awkwardness when they turn the pages of their e-books.

Amazon's engineers thought they solved the problem when they introduced the Kindle DX in 2009. The e-reader includes a tilt sensor, a feature found on tablet computers, smartphones, and other palm devices such as the Apple iPod Touch. Tilt sensors are also known as accelerometers, so-named because they measure the acceleration of gravity on the static electricity in the device. As the device is tilted, the accelerometer calculates the gravitational pull on the current and adjusts the screen to reflect the angle of view. It means that left-handed people can turn their devices upside down to read their e-books, thus placing the Kindle's Next Page button where they need it. Nonetheless, Pogue found Amazon's solution created a new problem. "Turning the DX upside-down is the only way to put Next Page near your left thumb," he says, "although, of course, now all the button names are upside-down, too."[38]

E-books in the Classroom

Complications such as where to place the Next Page button aside, Pogue has still found a lot to like about the Kindle DX and similar e-reader models. He has noticed, for example,

E-books Provide Relief for Sore Backs

California's move toward e-textbooks was prompted partly by economic reasons—the state spends more than $300 million a year buying textbooks for public school students—but state officials also acted out of concerns for young people's health. Studies show that many students suffer back injuries due to the weight of their backpacks.

A 1999 study by the U.S. Product Safety Commission found that some 3,400 students a year between the ages of five and fourteen seek treatment in hospital emergency rooms caused by the weight of their backpacks filled with heavy textbooks. A year later, a study by the Akron General Medical Center in Ohio found that 25 percent of students in the fourth and fifth grades typically carry backpacks weighing more than 20 percent of their body weights. In California, a 2004 report found most school backpacks weigh 40 pounds or more.

Former California governor Arnold Schwarzenegger, whose administra-tion approved the use of e-textbooks in 2009, says, "Number one, you don't have to carry around this heavy load in your bag, in your school bag, which my kids always complain about. And then, number two, I think it will help because you don't have to cut down as many trees. Think about that, how much paper is being used in those textbooks."

Quoted in *Current Events.* "Textbook Toss-Up." September 7, 2009, p. 7.

E-textbooks can offer relief to students overwhelmed with backpacks full of books.

that the screen of the DX—10.5 inches (26.7 cm) by 8 inches (20.3 cm)—is larger than prior Kindle models. He says, "The larger screen size was developed in anticipation of what could be e-books' killer [application]: textbooks."[39]

In fact, some students are already finding fewer textbooks in their backpacks thanks to the availability of e-books. E-books are much less expensive than hardbacks, and financially-strapped school districts are finding ways to make e-books available as textbooks to their students. By 2012, four states—Florida, Idaho, Utah, and California—established statewide programs to make e-book versions of textbooks available.

Educators believe young people have become so immersed in technology that e-textbooks will be a natural fit for them. "Our children live in a different world," says Sheryl Abshire, chief technology officer for the Calcasieu Parish School District in Louisiana. "We're going to have to step up smartly to meet their needs or we are going to be irrelevant to them, and I don't think that public education can afford to be irrelevant to [students]."[40]

Transitioning to Flexbooks

E-textbooks offer another advantage over printed textbooks—they can be more easily, and cheaply, updated than printed textbooks. This new trend in textbook publishing is known as *flexbooks*. The flexbook concept was started by the CK-12 Foundation, a nonprofit group based in Palo Alto, California, that produces e-textbooks by forming partnerships with university professors and authors who volunteer their time. The foundation has produced more than sixty e-textbooks, most in math and science, which can be downloaded by teachers and distributed to students.

Under the program, the textbook authors have agreed to update the content of the books from time to time. One au-

A high school teacher in Indiana demonstrates a Kindle. Some educators find e-readers are ideal for classroom use.

thor who joined the program is James Dann, a Menlo Park, California, high school science teacher who wrote his own e-textbook for his students titled *People's Physics*. "The book has evolved and flexed with students and with the evolution of the class, curriculum, and even physics," says Dann. "I was 100 percent onboard and donated *People's Physics* immediately."[41]

In addition, when using flexbooks in class teachers can alter the content, enhancing material for some students who are faster learners and simplifying the material for slower learners. "Students are coming to school with different skill sets," says Peter Noonan, assistant superintendent for Fairfax County Public Schools in Virginia. "We need to meet them where they are and use technology for learning."[42] Moreover, flexbooks can also be updated when the content needs to be updated—a common occurrence in history and political science classes, where changes in world events often make textbook content out-of-date, and in science classes, which often use textbooks that do not feature information on new discoveries.

School officials realize, though, that a conversion to e-textbooks could be a far from seamless transition. Certainly, a number of students own laptop computers, tablets, and e-readers that they can take to school with them—but many students are members of families that cannot afford the devices. That would mean the school districts would have to buy e-readers for students. Still, in 2012, U.S. Education Secretary Arne Duncan called on school districts to make the transition to e-textbooks. "Do we want kids walking around with 50-pound backpacks and every book in those backpacks costing $50, $60, $70 and many of them being out of date?" he asks. "Or, do we want students walking around with a mobile device that has much more content than was even imaginable a couple years ago and can be constantly updated? I think it's a very simple choice."[43]

A Minnesota middle school teacher shows a tutorial on how he taught his special education students to use the Kindle. Some of his students said that the Kindle motivated them to read more.

Do E-books Enhance Literacy?

Although flexbooks would seem to have many advantages over printed textbooks, there is one basic function that is common in both types of books: To be of any use to students, they have to be read. Many educators believe that if students are slow readers, e-textbooks may hold advantages that are lacking in printed books. In the California Leadership Public School Program, more than half of the ninth-grade students read at a fourth-grade level. To help them understand the concepts in their math and science books, teachers have altered the flexbooks to include literacy lessons. For example, teachers can alter the science flexbooks so that multisyllable scientific terms can be spelled out phonetically.

Laptop computers can be hooked to smartboards, enabling the contents of e-books to appear on large screens at the front of the classrooms. Educators have found that many elementary school students tend to pay more attention to the contents of an e-book when they are projected onto a wide screen, which helps enhance the graphics, illustrations, and other eye-catching features. Julie Hume, a reading specialist in University City, Missouri, projected an e-book onto a smartboard for slow readers in third-, fourth-, and fifth-grade classes and quickly saw how the images and words captured the attention of the students. "It gave me chills,"[44] she says.

Another way students can improve their academic skills through the use of e-readers stems from the wide availability of e-books—students do not have to wait until the school library opens to check out the e-books they need. E-books are typically available for downloading twenty-four hours a day, seven days a week. Such easy access to a collection of e-books could be particularly helpful to the student working on an assignment over the weekend and suddenly finding that he or she lacks an important resource. Without access to the library's e-book collection, the student would have to wait until the school library reopened to obtain the printed book.

Some reading experts agree that e-books can be an important resource for students, but they caution that e-books should not be the only source of literature for young readers. Gabrielle Miller, national executive director for the

READERS OF E-BOOKS READ MORE FREQUENTLY THAN OTHERS

Percentage of Americans age 16 and older who read every day or nearly every day for these reasons

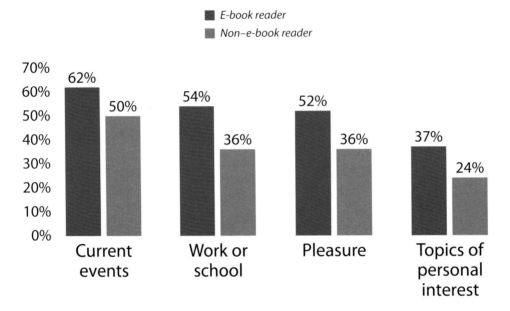

■ E-book reader
■ Non–e-book reader

N=2,986 respondents age 16 or older. Interviews were conducted in English and Spanish and on landlines and cells. The margin of error for the sample is +/-2 percentage points. N for e-book readers=739. N for non–e-book readers=1,681.

Mountain View, California–based foundation, Raising a Reader, which distributes picture books to families, says that at some point in their lives young readers are going to be handed print versions of books and expected to know how to read them. Printed books may lack the flash of e-books, she says, and therefore they may lose the attention of readers whose only reading experiences have been with e-books. "Without the balance of children holding and touching and learning how to take care of a book, you run the risk of children losing a sense of what books are and how they feel," she says. "You lose the understanding of how they came to be."[45]

New Reading Habits

There is no questioning the fact that e-books have greatly affected the way many people use books. Science fiction writer David Gerrold says he is astounded by the amount of information his e-reader has placed at his fingertips:

> Regardless of which ebook reader you end up with, the ebook has stopped being a curiosity or a novelty and become a serious player in the publishing industry. An ebook reader lets you carry around a whole library in one convenient package. You can carry around the latest bestsellers, old favorites, dictionaries, manuals, textbooks, all kinds of convenient references, and a lot of books that are no longer available in print editions. You can also download your own files to it, too. On my Kindle, I have manuals for the courses I teach, the text of a speech I will be giving later this year, some poetry, the manual for my camera, and test downloads of stories before I publish them on Amazon so I can check formatting.[46]

Readers who have found themselves hooked on e-books have grown accustomed to turning pages by pushing buttons or swiping their fingers across tablet screens. E-book enthusiasts have also learned to recognize that page numbers may not be accurate or even particularly relevant to their reading experiences. Perhaps students, above all other readers, will find that they have to develop new study habits. In the future, more students will find themselves studying from flexbooks or reading novels and nonfiction books in their e-book formats.

CHAPTER 4

How Are E-books Changing the Publishing Industry?

D arcie Chan is not a professional writer. She is a lawyer who helps draft environmental legislation for federal lawmakers. Years ago, answering the call of her muse, she wrote a novel titled *The Mill River Recluse* in her spare time. The book tells the touching story of a wealthy but troubled woman who locks herself away in her mansion and then bestows her fortune on the townspeople who barely knew her. Critics found the story enchanting. Wrote a critic for Kirkus: "Chan's sweet novel displays her talent. Sporting a complicated structure, it shifts back and forth between past and present and between various characters' perspectives—the author handles these changes with confidence and doesn't leave readers confused."[47] At the time that review was posted in 2011, readers could not find *The Mill River Recluse* in hardback or paperback versions in any bookstore or for sale through online booksellers. Over the years, Chan sent the manuscript to a dozen mainstream publishers as well as more than one hundred literary agents—professionals who represent authors and sell their manuscripts to publishers. All publishers and agents rejected the manuscript, which in the publishing world is common. Publishers and agents are routinely flooded with manuscripts by first-time and unknown authors. As a result, many talented authors miss their opportunities for success because their manuscripts languish along with the others in the *slush pile*—the industry's term for unsolicited manuscripts. "Nobody was willing to take a chance," Chan says. "It was too much of a publishing risk."[48] Chan was determined to break out of the slush pile. She could have self-published a print edition of the book, paying the cost of printing while attempting to sell the book on her own, but most self-published ventures rarely pay off. Graphic design and printing costs often run high and booksellers are reluctant to stock self-published books on their shelves, knowing that such books receive little publicity or other marketing efforts, which are vital to creating the buzz needed to sell books.

So Chan chose a different route. She self-published *The Mill River Recluse* as an e-book, making it available on Amazon for 99 cents. Within a few months of the e-book's release, *The Mill River Recluse* had gone viral, selling more than four hundred thousand copies.

The Speed of E-publishing

E-books have opened the floodgates to writers like Chan who found it hard to be accepted by the mainstream publishing industry. Indeed, anybody with a wish to become a novelist, poet, or nonfiction author can sit down at a computer, compose a book, and take advantage of widely available software that can turn their manuscripts into e-books. Moreover, Amazon and other online retailers have made their websites available to self-publishers who can name their prices, list their books for sale, and collect royalties when buyers download their books onto their tablets and e-readers.

By self-publishing their e-books, authors have complete creative control over their work. Authors can design their own covers and graphic content and decide when to release their books. According to the publishing trade journal *Book Marketing Update*, once an author finishes a manuscript, it typically takes a mainstream publisher twelve to eighteen months to release a print version of the book. On the other hand, e-books can be uploaded to the websites of online booksellers as soon as the authors finish the books and

Author Barry Eisler, a former technology attorney, has found success by e-publishing four anthologies of short stories.

format the manuscripts. "It's wonderful to be writing a book right now that my readers will have access to in a [short time], rather than 12 to 18 months from now," says author Barry Eisler, who has e-published four anthologies of short stories. "That, to me, is the single best aspect of this exciting time for authors."[49] It may take very little time for an e-book to hit the market, but it does not happen instantly—manuscripts composed with word processing programs must be formatted so they resemble books and can be read on e-readers and tablets. Photographs and illustrations may have to be displayed as well. A number of software designers have produced several programs that accomplish this task. A program in wide use is Adobe InDesign, which enables designers to create electronic pages featuring text and photos that resemble printed pages. To convert their Microsoft Word documents into e-book text, self-publishers often use the program Aspose.Words.

Secrets to Successful Formatting

If authors do not feel comfortable formatting their manuscripts on their own, they can turn to online services for help. One of the most popular online formatting services is Smashwords, which helps authors prepare manuscripts so they can be read on the Kindle, Nook, Sony Reader, and other devices. Smashwords also makes the e-books available to online booksellers. Smashwords has published its own e-book, the *Smashwords Style Guide*, which provides advice to authors:

> The secret to ebook formatting success is "Keep it Simple!" Unnecessarily complex formatting or layout will hinder the readability of your ebook. If you attempt to make your ebook an exact facsimile of [a] print book, you will cause yourself—and your readers—unnecessary frustration. It may also cause your ebook conversions to fail. Re-envision your book as free flowing text with only the essential formatting. Restrict your formatting to normal paragraph style for the bulk of your book, one paragraph return at the end of each paragraph, proper first line paragraph indents . . . italics, bolds, a heading style only for your chapter headings, and very few if any additional paragraph styles beyond that. Simple doesn't mean you can't use formatting, or you can't use styles. It just means that if your current formatting includes 15 or 30 different custom paragraph styles, you're asking for trouble.[50]

The *Smashwords Style Guide* illustrates the type of decisions e-publishers have to make if they expect to produce their e-books on their own. In Chan's case, after deciding that she would never find a mainstream publisher, she went through the steps to format *The Mill River Recluse* as an e-book. For the cover art, she found a photograph her sister had taken of an old mansion. Using the photo manipulation program Adobe Photoshop, Chan added graphics as well as a gloomy aura to the photo to create a

BITS & BYTES

30

Self-published authors who have sold more than one hundred thousand copies of their e-books through Amazon.com.

cover for the e-book. After converting the manuscript to an e-book format, she uploaded the package to Amazon as well as Barnes & Noble's online bookstore. She also decided to charge a mere 99 cents for the book—believing the low price would help boost sales. "I did that to encourage people to give it a chance," she says. "I saw it as an investment in my future as a writer."[51]

Creating Hype

When authors like Chan decide to e-publish, they also take on the responsibility of selling their books. Mainstream publishers will often buy advertising in magazines, newspapers, and websites, schedule authors for interviews, and send copies to book critics. These steps create hype for the book, which helps sell copies. Authors who e-publish, however, have to find ways to sell the books on their own. Chan spent about one thousand dollars buying ads for *The Mill River Recluse* on websites visited by e-reader owners.

In addition, a number of online book review services have emerged. These services, such as Kirkus, Blue Ink, and Indie Reader, charge fees to self-published authors (both print and e-book) and post the reviews on their websites. Chan paid for reviews of *The Mill River Recluse* on the Kirkus and Indie Reader websites, both of which praised the work.

The hype that Chan was able to create helped her sell downloads of *The Mill River Recluse*. Sales of the book started slowly—just one hundred copies were downloaded in the first month. As word spread across the Internet, more readers discovered the book. As Chan expected, the low price helped convince many readers to buy her book. In the second month, *The Mill River Recluse* sold 14,000 downloads and in the third month, 77,000 downloads.

By early 2012, *The Mill River Recluse* was still holding its ground among the top fifty bestselling e-book novels available through Amazon. Moreover, the mainstream publish-

Royalties for E-books

Bestselling authors can become very wealthy but most people who have published books hardly get rich from the royalties they collect on their work. Hardback publishers typically pay authors royalties of no more than 17.5 percent per book. It means that an author earns only about $4 for a hardback book that sells for $25. Paperback royalties are even lower—they often amount to no more than 7.5 percent.

A reason authors earn so little money per copy is that many other professionals must share in the profits from the book—including the publishers, printers, warehouse operators, trucking companies, bookstore owners, marketing experts, and others. Authors who self-publish their e-books can collect much higher percentages. The reason: They eliminate the costs of printing, and they market the books on their own.

Royalties vary among online booksellers, but according to the publishing industry journal *Book Marketing Update*, e-book authors can collect royalties as high as 85 percent on their books. Reports *Book Marketing Update*, "Can you make money through digital self-publishing, even if you're an unknown author? Absolutely. Ebooks have made great strides in leveling the playing field for authors."

Book Marketing Update. "Is Ebook Self-Publishing the Next Big Thing?" January 2012, p. 13.

ing industry had taken notice and by early 2012, Chan was weighing a number of offers from publishers to market her book in a print edition. In addition, a half-dozen movie producers have been in contact with Chan, making offers to buy the film rights for the book. As for Chan, she is stunned by the novel's success. "I had no idea how *Recluse* would be received, but I felt that I had done my best and hoped that at least some people would enjoy it," she says. "I have been flabbergasted and humbled by readers' response to my novel. *Recluse*'s popularity has truly come as a complete shock to me."[52]

A Huge Online Inventory

In less than a decade, the inventory of e-books has exploded. In 2011, Amazon announced that its e-book inventory included some 950,000 titles. Meanwhile, Barnes & Noble said that more than 1 million e-books are available for the Nook. Google has also expanded its e-book project beyond its free Google Books website and made the Google eBook service available to bookstores. Google eBooks makes full versions of e-books available for reading on tablets and other computers. Google eBooks has made some 4 million titles available for purchase through bookseller websites. Regardless of this growth, in 2011 e-books still represented just 10 percent of overall book sales in the United States—but they are the fastest-growing segment of the industry.

In 2010, e-books accounted for $263 million in sales—a 56 percent increase over sales in 2009.

There may be a lot of titles available for downloading but as online booksellers compete for customers, obtaining books can be something of a complicated undertaking. For example, online booksellers have built software restrictions that place restrictions on books e-reader owners may lend to friends who also own e-readers. Amazon, for example, places fourteen-day lending restrictions on many of its e-books if the publishers approve, and if the publishers refuse the books are not lendable at all. Nicholson Baker complains, "[Kindle books] are closed clumps of digital code that only one purchaser can own. A copy of a Kindle book dies with its possessor."[53]

Conflicts at the Library

Nowhere have these conflicts been felt more strongly than at public and school libraries, which have long desired to make e-book titles available to cardholders and students but have found themselves negotiating through tricky waters to make that happen. Typically, when a library obtains a new print book it permits the volume to remain on loan for three weeks, but libraries usually allow people to renew their books and many libraries enable their readers to renew online, meaning they do not have to go back to the library to check out the book again. Newly-published books—particularly very popular titles—may be limited to checkouts of two weeks or even less with no renewal options. Ultimately, though, printed books can be expected to remain on the shelves and in circulation, available to cardholders, for years.

When libraries obtain e-books for their collections, publishers have made them follow strict rules that limit their availabilities to readers. For starters, libraries are generally limited to a single copy of the e-book and permitted to download it to one cardholder at a time, only. When the cardholder is finished with the e-book in the allotted time—typically two weeks—he or she does not have to send it back electronically, as though the reader is returning a print copy. Instead, the book simply becomes inaccessible on the owner's e-reader or tablet—essentially, an internal timer in the e-book deletes it from the device. If the reader has not finished the book before the deadline, he or she is out of luck—there is no renewing. To finish the book, the reader has to download it again. If it is a popular book, there may be quite a wait—several months can go by before the reader reaches the front of the queue and the book is available again if, in fact, it is still available.

Many publishers have placed quotas on the number of times libraries may permit downloads of their titles—in 2011, the major New York publisher HarperCollins placed a twenty-six-download limit on its titles. Meanwhile, some publishers refuse to make their e-book titles available to libraries. Simon & Schuster, for example, has never sold its e-book titles to libraries while another publisher, Hachette Book Group, stopped making its titles available to libraries in 2009. "Selling one copy that could be lent out an infinite

A reference librarian in Brookline, Massachusetts, demonstrates some of the e-readers available at his library. Some institutions are eager to embrace e-books, but have been hampered by restrictions set by publishers.

number of times . . . is not a sustainable business model for us,"[54] says Maja Thomas, a senior vice president at Hachette.

Library administrators have bristled at the rules imposed by publishers. Many library administrators fear that as e-books become a more significant part of the reading experience, their inability to make e-books more widely available to their members will force them to become less relevant in their communities. "[The e-book market] is going bananas and is leaving us behind,"[55] says Sue Polanka, head reference librarian at Wright State University in Ohio.

Some librarians have taken steps to fight back. Brett Bonfield, director of the Collingswood Public Library in New Jersey and Gabriel Farrell, an information technology official for the library at Drexel University, have organized a campaign that calls on libraries to boycott HarperCollins books—both print and e-book versions—until the company ends its twenty-six-download policy. More than two hundred libraries in the United States have joined the boycott. Kate Sheehan, an information technology specialist for Bibliomation, an organization that coordinates e-book lending for Connecticut libraries, says, "Right now, [e-books are] just gravy, but at some point this is going to be how a lot of people are reading and this isn't a sustainable business model for reading. If [the twenty-six-download limit] becomes the precedent for the long-term it's going to be devastating for libraries."[56]

Fears of Online Piracy

HarperCollins and other publishers have adopted these policies in part because they fear online piracy—that downloaders will copy the titles and distribute them to friends over the Internet—or even sell them on an e-book black market. It is a legitimate concern—the piracy of copyrighted music and movies over the Internet has been a longstanding issue that has perturbed composers, performers, and film producers for several years, costing them tens of millions of dollars in lost royalties.

With the explosion of interest in e-books, piracy has become a true concern for book publishers as well. For example, when Dan Brown's novel *The Lost Symbol* hit the bookstores in 2010, it was an instant bestseller. It was also a hot download on Amazon, but twenty-four hours after its release as an e-book, authorities estimated that hackers distributed one hundred thousand pirated copies. "It's fair to say that piracy of ebooks is exploding,"[57] says Albert Greco, a professor of marketing at Fordham University in New York.

Clearly, publishers see libraries as a prime source of concern. With limited resources, publishers fear libraries cannot devote large budgets to anti-hacking technology. Many libraries obtain the software that enables them to procure e-books and make them available to members through OverDrive, an e-book distributor. Librarians at some small libraries admit they cannot afford the OverDrive software, which includes anti-hacking features. "We've investigated e-books and e-book readers and the cost, and it's quite expensive," says Sofia Kimsey, library services supervisor at the Oxnard Library in California. "OverDrive would cost several thousands of dollars for the platform for e-books. At this time, we don't have any funding set aside."[58]

The Death of Print?

Regardless of whether they can improve their access to e-books, libraries will still have access to books in print—which may place them a step ahead of some of the country's largest bookstore chains. In 2011, Borders, which operated more than five hundred bookstores in the country, went out of business. Borders maintained an online bookstore and sold e-books as well as Kobo e-readers; nevertheless, the company's core business was centered on the operation of bookstores and the sale of hardbacks and paperbacks.

Analysts said it was clear Borders was losing customers to Amazon and other online booksellers, and the company failed to make e-books a significant part of its business. *Bloomberg Businessweek* reporter Ben Austen walked through a Borders in suburban Nashville, Tennessee, as it was about to close, selling its remaining stock at 90 percent discounts. He wrote, "It was difficult in the stark

surroundings not to think of a battle waged and lost, of the armies of Kindle owners and e-book peddlers off celebrating victory while all around lay the carnage [of unsold books]."[59]

By 2011, Barnes & Noble appeared to be facing financial trouble as well. Barnes & Noble maintains an online store and also sells e-readers and e-books but, like Borders, its principal business is focused on operating bookstores—more than seven hundred nationwide—and selling print versions. In 2011, the company put itself up for sale and found no buyers, which at the time was regarded as an ominous sign for the nation's largest bookstore chain. However, in 2012 Microsoft bought a 17.6 percent share in Barnes & Noble's Nook division. With the financial muscle of Microsoft now behind the Nook, financial analysts predict Barnes & Noble will be in a better position to compete against Amazon for e-book sales—a circumstance that could benefit the whole company.

A Borders book store in California holds a going-out-of-business sale in 2011. Borders was a casualty of the changing book business.

Nevertheless, if a major bookseller like Borders was forced into extinction, then independent bookstores also find themselves challenged as they compete for business in a market that is becoming more and more devoted to e-books. P.K. Sindwani, proprietor of the Towne Book Center in Collegeville, Pennsylvania, says his bookstore had always been very profitable since the day he opened for business in 1990. By 2010, though, his store was barely breaking even. He was forced to find a location with cheaper

Price-Fixing and E-books

A 2012 U.S. Justice Department lawsuit alleged that some e-book publishers broke federal laws that prohibit price-fixing. By dictating prices, the agency says, the publishers restrained the right of retailers to compete for business by cutting prices. Three publishers, Hachette Book Group, Simon & Schuster, and HarperCollins, admitted to no wrongdoing but agreed to an immediate settlement—permitting retailers to set prices for e-books.

At the root of the case is the fairness of the *agency model*, in which publishers set prices for books. Two publishers that had not settled, Macmillan and Penguin Group USA, adopted the agency model claiming they took that step to compete with Amazon, the behemoth online bookseller that can cut e-book prices to a minimum and remain profitable. Another company sued by the U.S. Department of Justice was Apple, which is alleged to have conspired with publishers to set prices for books sold through the company's iBookstore site. In its response to the Department of Justice, Apple said that before establishing iBookstore, Amazon had the e-book market virtually to itself and, therefore, e-book prices were hardly competitive. Apple says, "Before [iBookstore], there was no real competition, there was only Amazon."

Quoted in Nick Wingfield. "Apple Strikes Back at Government E-book Lawsuit." *New York Times*, May 25, 2012. http://bits.blogs.nytimes.com/2012/05/25/apple-strikes-back-at-government-e-book-lawsuit.

rent and, to save money on the move, enlisted customers as volunteers to help transport his inventory. Sindwani blames e-books for his troubles—he has noticed many customers come into his store and browse through books without buying. He suspects they are *showrooming*, the industry's term for people who page through books in a bricks-and-mortar bookstore, then buy them online or as e-books. After making the move to his new location, Sindwani has added the Google eBook service to his store's website. Still, he believes independent booksellers face an uncertain future. "It's an industry where you don't feel secure, your head is spinning constantly,"[60] he says.

Print Books and E-books Can Coexist

Despite the fears of booksellers like Sindwani, many experts and others who are influential in the publishing business cannot imagine a future without printed books. Graydon Carter, editor of *Vanity Fair* magazine, says:

It's become fashionable to proclaim that print is dying, as if a medium that has been around for more than five centuries might, like a guest who has overstayed his welcome, suddenly glance about the room, see his hostess nodding off in her chair, and realize it's time to call it a night. . . .

As the monks who were put out of business by Gutenberg's printing press could have told you, technological innovation is nothing new. The telegraph put the Pony Express out of business after just 19 months of operation. There used to be a piano in most middle- and upper-middle-class homes. Once the record player and the radio came into being, the business of making pianos for home entertainment crumbled. E-mail is hurting snail mail. But not every media revolution ends with one combatant lifeless on the ground, blood trickling from his mouth.[61]

Indeed, Carter argues that e-books and print books can exist side by side and points to the explosion in the number of television sets found in people's homes during the 1950s. Until then, most people turned on their radios to find broadcasts of sports, entertainment, and news. However, he says, even though television has become a dominant presence in American life, there are still radios in most homes.

Merrill Distad, associate librarian of the University of Alberta in Canada, maintains that as publishers place constraints on library downloads of e-books, they could actually drive people to buy the print copies. He also argues that many people enjoy the physical act of owning their favorite books and seeing them on their bookshelves at home as a constant reminder that these books brought joy to their lives—a feeling that he imagines is lost when the books are secluded in an e-reader. He says, "When one stops to consider the drawbacks of e-books, they come up short by failing to deliver any of the aesthetic, tactile, olfactory or sensual pleasure offered by printed books."[62]

Whether books are read in print or on e-readers, desktops, laptops, or tablet computers, the act of what the user is doing with them has never changed nor will it ever change—he or she is still reading words, rendered in a typeface, that tell a story. If that were not the case, the medium at hand would not be a book—it would be something else, such as a video or an audio recording. Therefore, the book that people read ten or twenty years from now, whether it is in a print version or an electronic version, will remain—at its core—a book. In other words, the nation's reading teachers will not soon find themselves out of work. Information dispensed in the form of readable words is here to stay.

CHAPTER 5

How Will E-books and E-readers Change in the Future?

In the years since e-paper first came into use in 1999, the one problem that has vexed its designers is how to display the cover, graphics, and illustrations of a book in color. The pigments in the e-paper microcapsules come in two colors: black and white. That is acceptable for reading text, but many books include colorfully illustrated features. It means the owners of Kindles, Nooks, and other devices that employ e-paper are unable to enjoy the colors available in the print or tablet versions of the books.

The problem with making e-paper display color centers on the reflective properties of the substance. Since e-paper is engineered to reflect sunlight or artificial light, adding color filters to the screens cuts down on the amount of light absorbed or reflected by the pigments in the microcapsules. Therefore, with less light hitting the microcapsules the display turns dull and hard to read. "The vibrancy of the colors isn't what people are looking for," says Dan Leibu, chief technology officer for Rakuten's Kobo division, headquartered in Toronto, Canada. "People want color."[63]

Engineers are working on a fix, though, and many industry insiders predict that color e-readers will be the state of the art within a few years. One company that believes it has made a breakthrough is Qualcomm, the San Diego, California, technology corporation that specializes

Qualcomm's Mirasol Display, shown here at the Uplinq 2010 Conference in San Diego, California, is the first to introduce color to e-readers.

in semiconductors and wireless communications. In 2011, Qualcomm introduced a color screen named Mirasol. The Mirasol screen is composed of millions of tiny mirrors that reflect light. These tiny mirrors are sandwiched above a reflective film and below a glass pane. As electrical charges are applied to the glass, the distances between the glass and the film expand and contract, creating different wavelengths of light—red, blue, and green—that are reflected by the mirrors. The hues created by the wavelengths blend together to add color to the images visible on the screen.

The first e-readers featuring Mirasol color screens went on the market in 2012, mostly in Asian countries where they are employed in devices made by the electronics companies Kyobo of South Korea and Hanvon of China. "I played with the two e-readers and they both offer significant advantages over the existing [e-paper] Kindles and Nooks," says *PC Magazine* writer Sascha Segan, who reviewed both devices. "Color book pages . . . looked sharp, with subdued, but lovely colors."[64]

Meanwhile, E Ink has pursued an alternate technology. E Ink's plans include adding color filters to the microcapsules while adding an artificial source of light to the front of the screens to make the colors stand out. A big concern with this technology, though, is that the new front-lighting feature will drain the e-reader's batteries faster.

While advancements have been made, many experts predict that widespread sales of color e-readers for the U.S. market are still in the future.

Breaking with the Past

The introduction of color into e-reader screens illustrates one of the big changes in e-book technology that is likely to occur in the near future. Considering that the current generation of e-readers is less than a decade old, technology experts foresee big changes for books as devices that display e-books move into their next generations.

E-books are similar to books in print in that they both only display text and illustrations; however, many experts believe e-readers and tablets are capable of doing much more. In the future, devices could enable readers to pursue the information they find in the text further than simply what they read on their screens. "If tablets become more ubiquitous as a media consumption device, I think it's likely

Reviving the Audiobook

Audiobooks date back to the 1930s when the American Foundation for the Blind first produced phonograph records—the content of which was not music but books. The books were generally read by movie stars and other celebrities who volunteered for the project. In 1979, Sony Corporation produced the Sony Walkman, a small cassette tape player that could be used with earphones. The device was designed to play music, but publishers soon saw the value of recording books on tape and made many titles available to Walkman owners and similar portable tape devices. Later, portable CD players could also be used to access recorded books.

Audio books may again become widespread consumer products thanks to MP3 technology, which enables listeners to download and play music. MP3 software has been employed for books by Ohio-based Findaway World, which manufactures an MP3 player known as the Playaway. Each 3.5-inch (9cm) square device comes pre-loaded with a specific book, which cannot be erased and replaced by another title; however, the Playaway can hold about eighty hours of content, enough for an audio version of the complete book. In the days of books on tape, most titles were abridged because cassettes could hold only an hour or two of content. Given the price of the Playaway models, about $90 to $120, it is expected that libraries will make up the biggest market for the devices and lend them to members similar to how they lend books in print.

A Playaway—shown here with a copy of the nonfiction book Brotherhood of Heroes—*is a self-contained audiobook player. MP3 technology has improved audiobooks and may make them popular again.*

that a lot more e-books are going to encompass more than just the written word," says *Forbes* magazine technology writer Alex Knapp. He continues:

> Nonfiction e-books would probably include a lot more dynamic content—I can picture, for example, history books including links to original sources that can be

consulted at leisure. I can picture mystery novels including mock-ups of clues [and] witness interviews to help bring the reader into the story a little bit more. . . . I wouldn't be surprised to see dynamic content become more integrated into written stories themselves.[65]

In publishing, the concept is known as *transmedia storytelling*. In other words, the story is told through more than one form of media. The concept is not new. For decades, many movies have been based on popular books. To produce a movie from the book, the book is adapted by writers into a screenplay that tells the book's story, but using the platform of the movie screen to display the content. If the movie made use of an original screenplay, it was not unusual for the movie producer to commission a writer to produce a *novelization* of the film. The writer would adapt the screenplay into the form of a novel, and it would be sold to readers in a print version.

J.K. Rowling, author of the Harry Potter *book series, has embraced transmedia storytelling with her Pottermore website.*

The digital age has enabled authors to take transmedia storytelling a step further, making the concept more interactive. In the past, fans of a hot novel often had to wait years before the movie version was released. With e-books, transmedia storytelling can occur as they read the book. Readers may not be able to access a filmed sequence through the e-book, but there is other content available that print books cannot provide.

One author who has embraced the concept of transmedia storytelling is J.K. Rowling, author of the *Harry Potter* series. Rowling released the *Potter* series in an e-book format in 2011. Readers who buy the e-book versions can access Pottermore.com, a website created by the author. Using their computers or tablets, readers of the e-book versions can become Pottermore members and enter a virtual version of Hogwarts, the boy wizard's school, where they will find extra material not available in the book. For example, readers will find additional text providing Potter fans with insider information on how Rowling created the characters and her inspirations for places and plots. Readers can also create their own Pottermore pages, posting drawings and stories of their own.

Readers Become Fact-Checkers

Nonfiction authors can employ transmedia storytelling in their work as well, but those who do may find their books subject to an increased level of scrutiny. Dan Lansing, a product development specialist for Google eBooks, says such interactive features will force authors to become more devoted to accuracy once they know that virtually any reader can turn into a fact-checker. "Say you are trying to learn more about the Middle East, and you start reading a book, which claims that something happened in a particular event in Lebanon in 1981, where the author was using his view on what happened," Lansing says. "But actually his view is not what [really] happened. There's newspaper clippings on the event, there are other people who have written about it who disagree with him, there are other perspectives. The fact that all of that is at your fingertips and you can connect it together completely changes the way you do scholarship, or deep investigation of a subject. You'll be able to get all the world's information, all the books that have been published, all the world's libraries."[66]

It would seem the opportunities for readers to explore this type of content are endless. As Knapp says, a mystery novel could not only provide the description of the scene of the crime, but perhaps a three-dimensional image as well, giving the reader an opportunity to look for clues. Perhaps the e-reader or tablet could access an MP3 file, providing some mood music to set the tone for suspenseful portions of the book.

It is possible that biographies about pop stars could provide access to MP3 files as well—enabling readers to hear songs described in the book or even recorded interviews with the subjects of the biographies. An e-book version of a cookbook may not only provide a recipe, but a link to the author's website where a reader can find a video of the author preparing the meal. "So far, the ebook as a medium has been about the past," says science fiction author David Gerrold. "The ebook will . . . become something more than just a way to read books. It will become its own specific and unique way of creating and sharing experience. There's a lot of experimentation going on. I won't even try to predict the specifics, but I think the ebook—as a medium—could be a game-changer."[67]

Access to the Cloud

Some entrepreneurs have already taken steps toward combining text, video, and audio as part of the e-book experience. One version of this concept, known as Blio, was released in 2010. Blio was conceived by Ray Kurzweil, the computer engineer whose contributions to e-book technology also include development of the optical scanner. He has also helped develop text-to-speech software that enables computers to convert text to audio for the visually-impaired. Kurzweil designed the Blio software to run on desktop computers, laptops, and tablets as well as dedicated e-readers. Blio displays e-books in their familiar format—with text and graphics—but also provides Internet access so that readers can pursue additional information about the topic on the Web. "People want to do everything," says Kurzweil. "They want to watch their movies, they want to do all their computing, their e-mail on one platform. They don't want to take another device."[68]

A feature of Blio enables the user to turn on an audio mode, which allows the device to read the book to the user. As the words are spoken by the computer, they are highlighted in the text so a reader can follow along—a feature that young children who are just learning to read may find desirable. Blio even turns the pages for the child as he or she follows the story. Blio also makes use of cloud computing, in which information from the e-reader or tablet is stored in a remote database. (By 2012, several companies, including e-book

Cloud databases such as Apple's allow integration between multiple devices.

providers Amazon and Google, established cloud computing databases.) For Blio users, access to the cloud means they can read portions of their books on their home computers, place electronic bookmarks in the pages where they have left off, and then hours later continue reading their books on their smartphones or e-readers that they have taken to work or school. Jason Griffey, professor of library technology at the University of Tennessee at Chattanooga, says:

> The technology [of Blio] is the star, providing a multilayered approach to displaying a book to the reader. If you wish to see the book exactly as printed, you can do that, a boon for textbooks, children's books, cookbooks, and the like, where the display of the printed page itself is meaningful. Or, if you are on a device that doesn't handle the printed page properly, you can choose to reflow the text and display it on a smaller screen like the iPhone. You can even choose how to reflow the text, changing the margins, number of columns, and more.
>
> One of the best tricks that Blio has up its sleeve is the deep integration with audio, something you would expect from technology developed by Kurzweil. It keys audio to the text at the individual word level, highlighting the text as the audio is read to you either by a text-to-speech voice or a voice actor. In addition, it will sync your progress up to the cloud, allowing you to do things like read for a bit on your computer, then pick up your iPhone to continue reading, decide to listen for a while on your drive home, and then pop the book open on your laptop and have it known at every step in this process where you are in the book.[69]

The Blio Is Made for Students

Such features could give casual readers more opportunities to read, but Kurzweil says students are likely to benefit the most from Blio. E-textbooks that Kurzweil says he hopes will be available through Blio would feature embedded videos—an anatomy book for biology students, for example, may feature an animation explaining parts of the body that can be started with a mouse click or through touchscreen technology.

Students may find the e-textbooks including quizzes—by using their cursors, they can answer questions at the end of chapters, and know instantly how well they have absorbed the content of what they have just read. For other users, such as magazine readers, Blio could feature publications with video commercials rather than just print ads.

Kurzweil made Blio available as a free download in 2010, but by 2012 there was still little content beyond the e-book text available for the program. At this point, Kurzweil says, the developers of Blio are waiting for publishers to catch up with the software to produce the type of content that Blio and similar programs could offer users.

E-books and Social Networking

One interactive feature that is sure to become a bigger part of the e-book experience is the integration of social networking into e-reader technology. If a reader enjoys a book and knows a friend is also reading the book, e-readers and tablets will be able to network, giving each reader opportunities to share their thoughts on the content. "It's impossible to have a conversation about book publishing without hearing the term 'social media,'" reports *Publishers Weekly*. "The reasons are simple. Social media platforms attract readers and potential readers, many millions of them, to discuss what's important in their lives—from books to pets to politics."[70]

One company that has created a social networking platform for e-readers is Copia Interactive, based in New York City. The software available from the company enables readers to add their comments into the margins of their e-books. These comments are posted on Copia's network of e-readers and can be read by friends or anybody else who joins the network—just as friends and others can post comments on Facebook and other social networking sites. By 2012, Copia's software was available for the company's e-readers only, which are marketed under the names Ocean and Tidal. Copia executives have hopes that some of the more popular brands, such as Amazon's Kindle and Barnes & Noble's Nook, will recognize the value of social networking through e-books and adapt the software for their users.

According to the company, bringing a social networking capability to e-books could be particularly beneficial to students who use e-textbooks: students can compare notes on their assignments, and teachers can insert their comments as well into the e-textbook margins. In 2012, Copia took a major step toward accomplishing this goal when some nine hundred college bookstores agreed to market the Copia software. According to GoodReads.com, "The possibilities for study groups, for additional notes and discussions from course professors, and even from students using the same text at an entirely different college or university with a different professor are nearly limitless."[71]

Engaging with Authors

If readers can network with each other through their e-books, then it is also possible for them to network with the authors. Copia has introduced this concept, enabling authors to add margin notes to e-books after they have already been published. Authors can also answer questions from readers posed through e-reader and tablet connections. "The author can literally add notes and comments for his readers, even after publication, that contain tidbits of pertinent information such as what he was thinking when he wrote this scene or how this character was actually based on a specific person," reports GoodReads.com. "This anecdotal information can enhance the reading experience by giving the readers insight into the thought behind the art."[72]

This type of interaction with the author may be of particular interest to book club members. As people meet to discuss their favorite books, comments from the authors directed to their specific questions could certainly enhance the experience for the participants.

Copia Interactive promotes its wares at the 2010 International Consumer Electronics Show in Las Vegas, Nevada. The company has created software that adds a social networking platform to e-readers.

Reading E-books in Bed

E-readers were designed to be read under bright sunlight, but as e-readers evolve, most are likely to include features that enable them to be read in dim light as well. According to Barnes & Noble, developer of the Nook e-reader, about 64 percent of adults read in bed. Moreover, the company says, the most frequent complaints it receives about its e-readers come from the husbands and wives of Nook owners who cannot get to sleep because their spouses insist on using their e-readers in bed—which, of course, require overhead lights to be read.

In 2012, the company released a new version of the Nook that features a component known as GlowLight, a small light embedded in the device and controlled by a button. The user can use the button to adjust the brightness of the light. The company says GlowLight will not illuminate the room, providing just enough light for the screen to be read. Amazon, manufacturer of the Kindle, as well as other e-reader manufacturers, are also believed to be developing lights for their devices that will enable readers to use them under low-light conditions.

Bob Stein, head of the Institute for the Future of the Book, a New York City-based group that studies future applications for e-books, wonders whether book club members would even have to leave their homes to attend their meetings. "Book clubs could meet inside a book,"[73] he says.

Some publishers have found their readers are happy to interact with one another in different ways. Harlequin Enterprises, the well-known publisher of romance novels, has started delivering single chapters to readers that can be read on their smartphones. In other words, Harlequin is making e-books available in serial form—a concept that was popular years ago when such weekly magazines as *Saturday Evening Post* and *Life* serialized books. Harlequin has taken its serialized books a step further: Along with the chapters, the readers also receive quizzes about the characters and plots, games, and the ability to share their comments with other Harlequin readers about the current titles. University of Minnesota librarian Nancy K. Herther says, "Given the historic experiences of book clubs and other methods devised to share books, reading and ideas, social networking may provide a better model to explore in future product ebook development."[74]

A Personal Library

With all these options available to e-book readers, some experts have realized that many users will need ways to manage their e-reader and tablet contents, lest they become flooded with books that are inaccessible because the user

A man reads a novel on an iPad in a home library. A number of companies are developing software to organize personal e-book libraries.

cannot find them. Such management issues could become more relevant as e-reader memories expand, enabling readers to store perhaps thousands of titles on their devices. To remedy this problem, software designers are devising virtual libraries for e-readers and tablets, giving the owners many options to catalog their e-books and employ other functions that place the volumes more readily at their fingertips.

One such system is known as Calibre, which was developed by software designer Kovid Goyal. The Calibre software, which is free to users, enables e-reader and tablet owners to place books in categories—such as mystery and suspense, romance, and science fiction—just as they would find print books on the shelves at libraries. Calibre features a "Fetch News" function, employing an Internet connection to search for news stories, including critical reviews, about the e-books and their authors. These reviews can be read through tablets and other computers on the websites of origin or downloaded, converted into an e-book format, and read on e-readers. Calibre also includes a function that enables the users to find online booksellers who stock the titles they want, giving readers many options to shop. When the user finds the edition he or she wishes to purchase, Calibre will connect the reader to the vendor to facilitate the sale. "The best description for Calibre is it tries to be an iTunes for your e-books; a place for you to manage them, view them, read them, and sync them to your e-readers," says Griffey. "It's the Swiss Army Knife of e-book software."[75]

When an e-book is loaded into the Calibre software and a reader calls it up on his or her device, the reader will see a reproduction of the cover as well as information about the book, including its author, year of publication, and genre. Calibre users can also rate their books—the software enables them to provide personal ratings on a system of zero to five stars.

Calibre also provides several ways for owners to browse through their collections. For readers who are accustomed to judging books by their covers, the software will flip through images of the covers. Calibre also gives e-reader

Becoming a Library Information Technologist

Job Description: The library information technologist manages the computer systems for public and school libraries. Many U.S. libraries now lend e-books through their Internet connections and permit users to renew print books through their websites. The library information technologist is responsible for managing these library services.

Education: A minimum of a bachelor's degree in information technology is required, but a master's degree in library science is highly desired for professionals who want to specialize in managing a library's information needs.

Qualifications: Mathematics skills are essential because the information technology field requires professionals to install and troubleshoot software that is driven by algorithms, the mathematical formulas that compose computer code. Good math skills also develop logical thinking, which helps in problem-solving. Library information technologists should be good problem solvers and crisis managers.

Additional Information: The Library and Information Technology Association, a division of the American Library Association, is the professional trade group for library information technologists. The association provides scholarships for students as well as a job bank on its website (www.ala.org/lita) for professionals seeking employment.

Average Salary: About $69,000 a year.

and tablet owners other options to search for their books, providing menus that feature authors, genres, publishers, and books that have been given ratings by their readers. In other words, if the owner wants to browse through a list of his or her top-rated books, the menu provides that option.

E-books of the Future

Developments like Mirasol, Calibre, and Blio are already on their way toward revolutionizing the e-book which, still largely in its most basic form, has already provided a dramatic change in the publishing industry and the way people read and write books. Certainly, e-books have come a long way since they first surfaced as widely available sources of literature. Even so, the e-books people read today may bear little resemblance to the e-books people will read years from now. Certainly, e-books are expected to evolve in the future, just as the Egyptian papyrus scrolls of five thousand years ago evolved into the first books printed on the Gutenberg press, which in turn evolved into the hardback and paperback books that have dominated the world of literature for the past five centuries.

Such industry leaders as Jeff Bezos, the head of Amazon, predicts that the e-reader will one day become as common in U.S. households as television sets, radios, and washing machines. "This is the most important thing we've ever done," Bezos says of the development of the Kindle. "It's so ambitious to take something as highly evolved as the book and improve on it. And maybe even change the way people read."[76]

As e-books continue to move into the future, there are plenty of opportunities for innovation. Considering that a quarter-century ago, e-book content was limited to what could be squeezed onto a floppy disk and were impossible to read in bright sunlight, the fact that e-books have advanced as far as they have in such short a time is truly astounding.

NOTES

Introduction: Publishing's New Frontier

1. Quoted in Julie Bosman. "E-Readers Catch Young Eyes and Go in Backpacks." *New York Times*, February 11, 2011.
2. Quoted in Bosman. "E-Readers Catch Young Eyes and Go in Backpacks."
3. Cory Doctorow. "Ebooks: Neither E, Nor Books." February 12, 2004. http://craphound.com/ebooksneitherenorbooks.txt.

Chapter 1: Evolution of the E-book

4. Quoted in Alison Flood. "Michael Hart, Inventor of the EBook, Dies Aged 64." *London Guardian*, September 8, 2011. www.guardian.co.uk/books/2011/sep/08/michael-hart-inventor-ebook-dies.
5. Quoted in L. Wiener. "You Can Look It Up—On a Disk." *U.S. News & World Report*, November 19, 1990, p. 73.
6. L.R. Shannon. "A Book, of Sorts, in Your Pocket." *New York Times*, November 17, 1992, p. C6.
7. Walter S. Mossberg. "New Electronic Books Still Haven't Become Page Turners." *Wall Street Journal*, September 17, 1998, p. B1.
8. Quoted in Tony Bove. *Just Say No to Microsoft*. San Francisco: No Starch Press, 2005, p. 89.
9. Google. Mission Statement. www.google.com/about/company.
10. James Crawford. "The Present and Future of Google Books." Books Online 2010, October 26, 2010. http://research.microsoft.com/en-us/events/booksonline10/keynotes.aspx.
11. Crawford. "The Present and Future of Google Books."
12. Quoted in Juan Carlos Perez. "Google Plans to Seek Books Lawsuit Dismissal." *PC World*, December 5, 2011. www.pcworld.com/article/245501/google_plans_to_seek_books_lawsuit_dismissal.html.
13. Quoted in Flood. "Michael Hart, Inventor of the Ebook, Dies Aged 64."

Chapter 2: The E-reader Revolution

14. Quoted in J. Gorman. "New Device Opens Next Chapter on E-Paper." *Science News*, April 28, 2001, p. 262.

15. Quoted in Associated Press. "New Ink Won't Rub Off Because It's Electronic: Newspapers and Signs Would Not Be Set in Stone." *Orlando Sentinel*, December 13, 1998, p. A24.

16. Quoted in Kim Honey. "Beyond Paper: Physicist Nick Sheridon's Goal Is to Make What You Are Now Holding in Your Hands a Thing of the Past." *Toronto Globe and Mail*, March 6, 2001.

17. Quoted in Lisa Guernsey. "Beyond Neon: Electronic Ink." *New York Times*, June 3, 1999, p. 11.

18. Lori Bell, Virginia McCoy, and Tom Peters. "Ebooks Go to College," *Library Journal*, May 1, 2002, p. 44.

19. Bell, McCoy, and Peters. "Ebooks Go to College," p. 44.

20. Paul Hilts, Calvin Reid, and Jim Milliot. "The Wait for an Ebook Format." *Publishers Weekly*, November 6, 2000, p. 55.

21. Quoted in Charles C. Mann. "Electronic Paper Turns the Page." *Technology Review*, March 2001, p. 42.

22. Phred Dvorak. "Electronic Readers, Now on Sale in Japan, Still Don't Beat Paper." *Wall Street Journal*, July 15, 2004, p. B1.

23. Dvorak. "Electronic Readers, Now on Sale in Japan, Still Don't Beat Paper," p. B1.

24. Quoted in Steven Levy. "The Future of Reading." *Newsweek*, November 26, 2007, p. 54.

25. Quoted in *USA Today*. "Amazon Hopes to Kindle Readers' Interest in Electronic Books." November 20, 2007, p. 3B.

26. Quoted in David Pogue. "Steve Jobs on Amazon and Ice Cream." *New York Times*, September 9, 2009. http://bits.blogs.nytimes.com /2009/09/09/in-qa-steve-jobs -snipes-at-amazon-and-praises -ice-cream.

27. Quoted in Levy. "The Future of Reading," p. 56.

Chapter 3: How Are E-books Changing the Way People Read?

28. Quoted in Levy. "The Future of Reading," p. 56.

29. Quoted in Matt Richtel and Claire Cain Miller. "Of Two Minds About Books." *New York Times*, September 2, 2010, p. B1.

30. Quoted in Richtel and Miller. "Of Two Minds About Books," p. B1.

31. Quoted in Richtel and Miller. "Of Two Minds About Books," p. B1.

32. David Pogue. "Page Numbers for Kindle an Imperfect Solution." *New York Times*, February 8, 2011. http:// pogue.blogs.nytimes.com/2011 /02/08/page-numbers-for-kindle -books-an-imperfect-solution.

33. Alexandra Horowitz. "Will the E-book Kill the Footnote?" *New York Times*, October 9, 2011, p. 39.

34. Peter Meyers. "Notes That Don't Break the Reading Flow." *O'Reilly Radar*, July 14, 2011. http://radar .oreilly.com/2011/07/footnotes -endnotes-digital-text.html.

35. Pogue. "Page Numbers for Kindle an Imperfect Solution."
36. Nicholson Baker. "A New Page." *New Yorker*, August 3, 2009, p. 24.
37. Baker. "A New Page," p. 24.
38. David Pogue. "The Kindle DX: Bigger, but with a Lot of Footnotes." *New York Times*, July 2, 2009. http://pogue.blogs.nytimes.com/2009/07/02/the-kindle-dx-bigger-but-with-a-lot-of-footnotes.
39. Pogue. "The Kindle DX: Bigger, but with a Lot of Footnotes."
40. Quoted in Rebecca Hill. "Turning the Page: Forget About Those Bulky Backbreakers, Digital Textbooks Are the Future." *School Library Journal*, October 1, 2010. www.schoollibraryjournal.com/slj/home/886880-312/turning_the_page_forget_about.html.csp.
41. Quoted in Hill. "Turning the Page: Forget About Those Bulky Backbreakers, Digital Textbooks Are the Future."
42. Quoted in Hill. "Turning the Page: Forget About Those Bulky Backbreakers, Digital Textbooks Are the Future."
43. Quoted in Kimberly Hefling. "Challenge to Schools: Embracing Digital Textbooks." *ABC News*, February 1, 2012. http://abcnews.go.com/Politics/wireStory/challenge-schools-embracing-digital-textbooks-15490068.
44. Quoted in Lisa Guernsey. "Are Ebooks Any Good?" *School Library Journal*, June 1, 2011. www.schoollibraryjournal.com/slj/printissuecurrentissue/890540-427/are_ebooks_any_good.html.csp.
45. Quoted in Guernsey. "Are Ebooks Any Good?"
46. David Gerrold. "Future Tense: The Ebook Also Rises." *Maximum PC*, March 30, 2011. www.maximumpc.com/article/future_tense_ebook_also_rises.

Chapter 4: How Are E-books Changing the Publishing Industry?

47. Kirkus. "The Mill River Recluse." July 21, 2011. www.kirkusreviews.com/book-reviews/darcie-chan/the-mill-river-recluse/#review.
48. Quoted in Alexandra Alter. "How I Became a Best-Selling Author." *Wall Street Journal*, December 9, 2011. http://online.wsj.com/article/SB10001424052970204770404577082303350815824.html.
49. Book Marketing Update. "Is E-book Self-Publishing the Next Big Thing?" January 2012, p. 12.
50. Mark Coker. *Smashwords Style Guide: How to Format Your Ebook*. Los Gatos, California: Smashwords, 2011. Kindle Edition.
51. Quoted in Alter. "How I Became a Best-Selling Author."
52. Quoted in Christopher Meeks. "Interview with Best-Selling Novelist Darcie Chan." *Red Room*, September 6, 2011. http://redroom.com/member/christopher-meeks/blog

/interview-with-best-selling-novel
ist-darcie-chan.

53. Baker. "A New Page," p. 24.

54. Quoted in Randall Stross. "Publishers vs. Libraries: An Ebook Tug of War." *New York Times*, December 25, 2011, p. BU3.

55. Quoted in Andrew Albanese. "Librarians Brace for a Tough 2011." *Publishers Weekly*, January 17, 2011, p. 4.

56. Quoted in Ki Mae Heussner. "Librarians Boycott HarperCollins Over Ebooks." *ABC News*, March 8, 2011. http://abcnews.go .com/Technology/librarians-boy cott-harpercollins-books/story?id =13084735.

57. Quoted in Matt Frisch. "Digital Piracy in the Ebook Industry." CNN, January 1, 2010. http://ar ticles.cnn.com/2010-01-01/tech /ebook.piracy_1_ebooks-digi tal-piracy-publishing-industry ?_s=PM:TECH.

58. Quoted in Anne Kallas. "E-books Growing in Popularity at Public Libraries." *Ventura County Star*, October 16, 2011. www.vc star.com/news/2011/oct/16/e books-growing-in-popularity-at -public.

59. Ben Austen. "The End of Borders and the Future of Books." *Bloomberg Businessweek*, November 10, 2011. http://businessweek.com/mag azine/the-end-of-borders-and-the -future-of-books-11102011.html.

60. Quoted in Maria Panaritis. "Bookstore Owner's Survival Fight." *Phil-*
adelphia Inquirer, April 22, 2012, p. C2.

61. Graydon Carter. "Print is Dying . . . Really?" *Adweek*, March 31, 2010. www.adweek.com/news/advertis ing-branding/opinion-print-dying -really-102951.

62. Merrill Distad. "The Future of Print: The Book." *Feliciter*, 2001, p. 183.

Chapter 5: How Will E-books and E-readers Change in the Future?

63. Quoted in Stu Wood. "E-Readers' Color Challenge." *Wall Street Journal*, July 15, 2011. http://online.wsj .com/article/SB10001424052702 3042238045764462634848396 94 .html.

64. Sascha Segan. "Qualcomm's Mirasol Display Could Mean New Color Nooks and Kindles." *PC Magazine*, February 28, 2012. www.pcmag .com/article2/0,2817,2400889,00 .asp.

65. Alex Knapp. "What Is the Future of the E-Book?" *Forbes*, April 4, 2011. www.forbes.com/sites/alex knapp/2011/04/04/what-is-the -future-of-the-e-book.

66. Quoted in Levy. "The Future of Reading," p. 56.

67. Gerrold. "Future Tense: The Ebook Also Rises."

68. Quoted in Ina Fried. "Ray Kurzweil Tries to Build a Better E-Reader." CNET, January 7, 2010. www.cnet .com/8301-31045_1-10428479 -269.html.

69. Jason Griffey. "Electronic Book Readers." *Library Technology Reports*, April 2010, p. 17.

70. Calvin Reed. "Adoption of Social Media Marketing Accelerates." *Publishers Weekly*, January 3, 2011, p. 19.

71. Mercy Pilkington. "Copia Brings Social Capability to Digital Textbooks." GoodReads.com, January 27, 2012. http://goodereader.com/blog/electronic-readers/copia-brings-social-capability-to-digital-textbooks.

72. Mercy Pilkington. "Copia Takes Social Reading to the Next Level." GoodReads.com, May 24, 2011. http://goodereader.com/blog/e-reader/copia-takes-social-reading-to-the-next-level.

73. Quoted in Levy. "The Future of Reading," p. 56.

74. Nancy K. Herther. "The Ebook Reader Is Not the Future of E-books." *Searcher*, September 2008, p. 26.

75. Griffey. "Electronic Book Readers," p. 19.

76. Quoted in Levy. "The Future of Reading," p. 56.

copyright: Law that protects the rights of authors and their heirs to profit from intellectual content, including books. Copyright law generally protects intellectual content for the lifetime of the author plus seventy years.

e-book: A book that has been converted to electronic format, enabling readers to access the text in a variety of devices, including tablet computers, e-readers, and smartphones.

e-paper: An oil-based substance containing millions of tiny capsules composed of black and white pigments; when an electrical charge is transmitted to the capsules, they form readable text.

e-reader: A device specifically devoted to displaying the text of e-books.

flexbook: An e-textbook that enables teachers and authors to change the text and customize it for students.

floppy disk: One of the first mediums used for data sharing, which enabled computer owners to swap information. Some of the first e-books were made available on floppy disks.

liquid crystal display: A medium employed for displaying text on early e-readers; the technology is based on transmitting electrical charges into crystals suspended in a liquid environment. LCD is still used for some e-readers and other products, such as digital thermometers.

location numbers: A system used by many e-readers as a substitute for page numbers; the reflowable text component of e-paper does not follow the original format of an e-book, making page numbers irrelevant.

microprocessor: Also known as the integrated circuit or silicon chip, the component of a computer that stores information and provides the computer with its ability to process data and carry out functions.

optical scanner: A device that converts images on a printed page into electrical impulses that are accepted by a computer and converted back into visual images that can be read on the computer screen.

portable document format: Also known as PDF, one of the first software programs that displayed the text of a book. PDFs can display text, graphics, and illustrations on computer screens.

public domain: Term applied to intellectual property, including books, in which copyrights have expired, giving anyone the right to republish the works. Legal experts have declared that books published prior to 1923 are in the public domain.

tablet: Hand-held computer capable of performing a number of tasks, including the display of e-books.

touchscreen technology: Process used to send commands to a tablet; touchscreens include layers under their glass screens that interpret pressure applied by fingers.

word processing program: Software that enables writers to create documents and manuscripts; the program provides users with widespread abilities to edit their work, identify spelling and grammar errors, and change the type size and fonts.

Books

Walter Isaacson. *Steve Jobs*. New York: Simon & Schuster, 2011. This biography about the co-founder of Apple covers Steve Jobs' role in the development of the personal computer and ultimately the iPad, the first commercially successful tablet computer.

Martyn Lyons. *Books: A Living History*. Los Angeles: J. Paul Getty Museum, 2011. Lyons, a professor of history at the University of New South Wales in Australia, traces the history of books from the papyrus scrolls of the Egyptians some five thousand years ago to the emergence of e-books in the twenty-first century.

Periodicals

Nicholson Baker. "A New Page." *New Yorker*, August 3, 2009. A novelist provides his mostly negative, but humorous, reactions to using the Kindle.

Vannevar Bush. "As We May Think." *The Atlantic*, July 1945. In this article, published more than sixty years ago, the scientist who helped develop the atomic bomb predicts that, in the future, a relatively small machine would be able to hold the contents of an entire library.

Jason Griffey. "Electronic Book Readers." *Library Technology Reports*, April 2010. A professor of library technology at the University of Tennessee at Chattanooga provides a comprehensive guide to using several of the most common e-readers on the market, including the Kindle, Nook, and Sony Reader. He also discusses future developments in e-reader technology, such as Blio, Mirasol, and the interactive features pioneered by Copia.

Websites

Calibre (http://calibre-ebook.com). This website provides free software for e-reader owners to help them manage their personal libraries and catalogue their books by cover, author, or genre.

Google Books (http://books.google .com/intl/en/googlebooks/about .html). This website explains the Google Books project, which aims to scan some 130 million books and make them available on the Internet. Visitors can read a history of the project as well as essays by authors supporting the project.

Institute for the Future of the Book (www.futureofthebook.org). Sponsored by the University of Southern California, the institute's website features essays by scholars who comment on the future of literature.

Project Gutenberg (www.gutenberg .org). Started more than forty years ago by University of Illinois student Michael Hart, Project Gutenberg remains a definitive source for public domain e-books. Visitors can browse through a library of some thirty-eight thousand books available for downloading.

Publishers Weekly (www.publishers weekly.com). This website is maintained by the national trade journal of the publishing industry. Visitors can find news covering the development of new e-readers, publication of new e-books, and interviews with authors and publishing industry insiders on e-publishing.

INDEX

A

Accelerometers, 60
Adobe (company), 26, 27, 70, 71
Agency model, 80
Amazon (online retailer)
    Adobe and, 27
    agency model and, 80
    Bezos, Jeff, and, 43–44, 45, *45*, 50, 98
    Borders and, 78
    sales, 12
    self-publishing and, 69
    smartphones and, 54
    See also Kindle
American Foundation for the Blind, 86
Apple (company)
    cloud computing, *90*
    iBooks 2, *55*
    iPod touch, 60
    personal computers, 19, 47–50
    price-fixing and, 80
    software, 20
Aspose.Words, 70
Association of American Publishers, 30
Atari, 19
Audiobooks, 86
Authors Guild, 29–30

B

Barnes & Noble, 27, 44, 50, *74*, 79
    See also Nook
Batteries, 38–39, 42–43
Bezos, Jeff, 43–44, 45, *45*, 50, 98
Bible, 14, 16, 22–24, 26, 33, 50

BlackBerry, 48
Blio, 89–92, 98
Blue Ink, 72
Bookman, 24, 33, 35, *38*
Borders (retailer), 44, 78, *79*
Brin, Sergey, 28, *31*
Brown, Dan, *42*, 43, 78
Bush, Vannevar, 15

C

CAD (computer-aided design), 46
Calibre (software), 96, 98
California Leadership Public School
    Program, 65–66
Cambridge Display Technology (CDT), 37
Capacitive screens, 48, 49, *49*
CD-ROMs, 23–24
Charged couple devices (CCDs), 18
Chin, Denny, 32
CK 12 Foundation, 62
Cloud computing, 89–91
Commodore (company), 19
Copia Interactive, 92–93, *92*
Copyright law, 27–32
Cover design, 69, 71–72
Crawford, James, 29, 30

D

Da Vinci Code (Brown), 43
Data sharing, 20, 23
Dictionaries, 20–21, 50
Digital age, 11, 88
Digital Book System, 24

PICTURE CREDITS

ABOUT THE AUTHOR

A former newspaper reporter and columnist, Hal Marcovitz has written more than 150 books for young readers. His other titles for Lucent include *The History of Music Videos* and *Sports Injuries*. He lives in Chalfont, Pennsylvania.